Date Due

FEB 13 2003			

ZUNI

and the

American Imagination

ZUNI

and the

American Imagination

—◆—

ELIZA McFEELY

—◆—

Ⓦ HILL AND WANG

A division of Farrar, Straus and Giroux

New York

Hill and Wang
A division of Farrar, Straus and Giroux
19 Union Square West, New York 10003

Library of Congress Cataloging-in-Publication Data
McFeely, Eliza, 1956–
    Zuni and the American imagination / Eliza McFeely.— 1st ed.
    p. cm.
    Includes bibliographical references and index.
    ISBN 0-8090-2707-0 (alk. paper)
    1. Zuni Indians.   2. Stevenson, Matilda Coxe, 1850–1915.
    3. Cushing, Frank Hamilton,1857–1900.   4. Culin, Stewart, 1858–1929.
    5. Intercultural communication.   6. Zuni Indians—Public opinion.
    7. Public opinion—United States.   I. Title.

E99.Z9 M24 2001
978.9'004979—dc21
                                                                00–063218

Permission to publish from papers in their collections has been granted by
the Brooklyn Museum and by the American Philosophical Society.

Designed by Jonathan D. Lippincott

For Jeff, Maggie, and Clara

CONTENTS

PREFACE

—◦◦◦—

This is a book about a society of Native Americans, the Zunis, that existed centuries before there was a United States. In the latter years of the nineteenth century, as people from the United States sifted and surged into spaces on the continent to which they had hitherto been strangers, they came up to the edge of this small agricultural community in the desert of what later became New Mexico. The sheer size of the culture that pulled up to Zuni's borders was staggering, and that larger culture's restless inhabitants had behind them political, military, and economic organizations, not to mention technology, so much more powerful than those of Zuni that they might easily have crushed the pueblo. Instead, though the confused juggernaut of American civilization that hovered around Zuni did plenty of damage, Zuni endured. But it did more than just survive. In part because of who and what Zuni was, and in part because of the way in which the United States reached it, Zuni exerted its own quiet influence at the edges of American consciousness.

With a history of interaction with the United States that contains all the elements of tragedy and comedy one might expect,

Zuni has long intrigued Americans. In the 1930s, Aldous Huxley, the English novelist who migrated to the United States, darkly reimagined *The Tempest*, Shakespeare's tale of exile and redemption. In *Brave New World*, he cast as his Miranda a child of London who is exiled in a pueblo that is a bleak futuristic projection of Zuni. That child, John Savage, reared among fictional descendants of the Zunis, educates himself by reading a volume of *The Collected Works of William Shakespeare* that someone has left behind in one of the pueblo's kivas. Repatriated to London, he draws on both Shakespeare and Zuni to articulate what is wrong with the engineered utopia London has become.

In the same decade, distressed by the wastefulness of the pointless world war that had devastated Europe between 1914 and 1918 and troubled by the political possibilities that now seemed to be taking shape, the anthropologist Ruth Benedict imagined Zuni in her best-selling *Patterns of Culture* as a communal, emotionally moderate alternative to the individualism and emotional excess of Western civilization. And, more recently, Robert Heinlein, a cult hero of American science fiction, played with Benedict's vision of an Apollonian Zuni, adapting it to the Martian counterculture at the heart of his novel *Stranger in a Strange Land*. His variation on *The Tempest*'s theme of savagery and civilization, published in 1961, remains a classic of the genre. In the decades since, Zuni has continued to attract the attention and excite the imagination of serious cultural anthropologists, tourists, and New Age pilgrims.[1]

Zuni was not the only native culture that inspired the projection of passionate hopes and fears, as well as more playful emotions, on the part of people of European descent. And many, if not most, readers of Huxley or Heinlein would neither know nor care that their fictionalized worlds had Zuni at their heart. But the fact is that the Zunis, a people long subjected to and too often derided by the larger culture that surrounds them, have maintained a grip on the imagination of intellectuals who are concerned with the legacy of that larger culture. Like the proverbial grain of sand in the oyster, Zuni lies at the core of these cultural creations. It has had an influence on the world outside its borders that is worth looking into.

This is a close look at three early anthropological visitors to Zuni, people whose work there provided the foundation for subsequent, better-known attempts to understand both Zuni and its relationship to the world around it. Matilda Stevenson, Frank Hamilton Cushing, and Stewart Culin studied Zuni at a moment that seemed full of big changes, both for Zuni and for America. The more I, in turn, studied them, the more intrigued I became with the capacity of anthropology to act as a mirror, reflecting back the cultural certainties and uncertainties of the anthropologists as they chronicled those of their subjects. The study of humankind is always on some level the study of ourselves; this study of Zuni has helped me to learn about Zuni and about the United States—and it has helped me to recognize my own face in the glass surrounding the Indian exhibits that I haunted as a child and continue to seek out. Our fascination with Zuni is still a fascination with ourselves.

ACKNOWLEDGMENTS

—◈—

So many people have had a hand in the making of this book that it is difficult to know where to begin to say thank you. Many archivists and historians took the time to help me: Deborah Wythe at the Brooklyn Museum; Belinda Kaye at the American Museum of Natural History in New York; Martin L. Levitt and Beth Carroll-Horrocks at the American Philosophical Society, which granted me a Mellon fellowship so that I could work in the Elsie Clews Parsons Papers; Mario Nick Klimiades and Kathleen L. Howard at the Heard Museum in Phoenix; Orlando Romero of the Museum of New Mexico's History Library; Janice Klein, Nina Cummings, and Ben Williams at the Field Museum in Chicago; and the staff at the Chicago Historical Society. Ira Jacknis of Berkeley's Lowie Museum took the time to answer many of my questions, as did Lea McChesney of Harvard's Peabody Museum. The Smithsonian Institution granted me a fellowship that allowed me to work in its archives: the National Anthropological Archives at the National Museum of Natural History, and the Smithsonian Archives in the Arts and Industries Building, the first United States National Museum. There I was assisted by unfailingly helpful and interested staff members. The fellowship also placed me among the extraordinary community of scholars gathered at the National Museum of American History. The museum staff has made the museum a lively national center of intellectual activity, ably carrying on the tradition established at the Smithsonian more than a century ago.

The History Department at New York University helped further my work with more-than-generous financial support and, more important, with intellectual support. Thomas Bender and Susan Ware offered invaluable help throughout the long process of the dissertation and continued to offer sage advice as I turned it into a book. Other scholars, too, gave careful attention to the manuscript, and this is a better book for the insights of Dorothy Nelkin, Walter Johnson, Charlie McGovern, and Michael O'Malley. Daniel Rodgers, Hendrick Hartog, and Christine Stansell, from the Princeton History Department, read all or parts of it and helped me see what it might be, and a research grant from Princeton University helped fund some of my research. Linda Kerber, one of the most generous intellectuals I know, read the manuscript for fun and provided inspiration at a moment when it was much needed. I was the recipient of much good advice; any errors that remain are mine alone.

If it takes a village (or a township) to raise a child, it takes something as intensive, if more far-flung, to write a book. I did both at the same time, and my two villages came together. If I hadn't had a brand-new baby and an old Berkshire Conference T-shirt, I might never have met two of my favorite historians, Lynn Mahoney and Grace Elizabeth Hale, both of whom influenced my work significantly. They have traveled with me on this project since its inception, as have an extraordinary group of scholars who have lent me both their expertise and their friendship at crucial junctures. Sally Charnow, Alice Fahs, Jeanne

Houck, and Diane Sommerville were perpetual sources of critical insight and moral support. Lola Van Wagenen, a historian, and Janet Webster, a banker with good historical sensibilities, each devoted considerable time to reading an early draft from start to finish, and both offered vital insights at that daunting moment when I began to think not only about the history but about the art of this book.

Closer to home, I had the support of a wonderful township full of people who provided a network of support for my family that made it possible for me to find that "room of one's own" essential to a project like this. From an obstetrician who majored in history to a PTA president who remembered to ask about the book even as she mobilized forces to pass a school budget, I was surrounded by a community I would not trade for the world. I can't thank them all by name, but I would be remiss if I didn't mention Kim Howarth and the staffs at the Ring Nursery and at Parkway School, as well as all the other extraordinary people in Ewing and the folks at the U.S. Geological Survey, who inspired and encouraged this book in ways they may not be aware of.

My family—Fischers, McFeelys, Goodmans, Tinos, and McLeans—have been wonderful; there are few families, I suspect, that can offer as much in the way of both moral support and professional advice. Each of my parents, Mary Drake McFeely and William McFeely, both of whom are historians, read this manuscript carefully more than once, in addition to supplying all the encouragement I could use whenever I needed it. It is a rare thing to have parents who are colleagues and can fill both roles at once. Equally rare was the attention Elisabeth Sifton, my editor, gave to my manuscript. This is a much tighter, much better book for her careful attention, and for that of the others at Hill and Wang who have helped to see the project through.

Finally, this book is for my husband, Jeff, and my daughters,

ACKNOWLEDGMENTS

Clara and Maggie, who kept it all going in numerous ways. People sometimes ask me how I managed to write a book and have a family at the same time. I couldn't have done one without the other.

Eliza McFeely
Ewing, New Jersey, 2000

ZUNI

and the

American Imagination

One

FINDING ZUNI

———ᴡᴡᴡ———

"O brave new world, / That has such people in't!" muses Shake-speare's Miranda as she gazes for the first time on other people of European descent. She speaks to her father, Prospero, who has to a large extent "gone native." " 'Tis new to thee," he replies, smiling sadly, for he knows the history of this Spanish branch of the human family. In *The Tempest*, civilization is brought to an iso-lated, untamed land to purge it of its excesses and to set things right again for its return to Europe. In addition to the familiar morality play, Shakespeare offered his audience, in the mis-shapen Caliban, a glimpse of the strange inhabitants of the mys-terious continent across the Atlantic that had begun, in the late sixteenth century, to excite the European imagination. Here was an inversion of what civilization should mean, a dark, cruel other against whom Europeans of birth and refinement might measure and confirm their own accomplishments.[1] And, in the idea of an exiled child of civilization who casts a fresh eye over its claims, he lit a creative spark that has continued to inspire authors, social critics, and audiences.

This fantasy of Spaniards at large in the New World had a basis in reality that had already stretched back a century or more when Shakespeare wrote *The Tempest* in 1611. On the heels of Columbus, the Spanish had invaded and ruthlessly conquered the empires of the Aztecs and the Incas, set to work extracting what precious metals they could find, and restlessly looked around for other lands and peoples that might yield similar wealth. Wonder at the sophistication of the societies they encountered mingled with age-old romances of lost cities and a powerful desire to believe in untold riches. One such romance attached itself to the Seven Cities of Cíbola. Spanish memories of a medieval legend about seven wealthy Christian cities somewhere in the Atlantic seemed to be echoed in stories the Aztecs told of seven caves that might be found along their trade routes to the north. Inspired by the extraordinary worlds they had already discovered in what is now Mexico and Peru, Spaniards in search of new conquests pushed north along the Pacific coast, but they found neither golden cities nor treasure caves.

Then, in 1528, a Spanish ship was wrecked off the coast of Florida. Two survivors wandered inland, like the shipwrecked Spaniards in Shakespeare's play. For a decade they made their way west across the continent, arriving at last at a Spanish settlement at Culiacán, on the Pacific coast. Along the way, they encountered people who told them of cities to the north whose inhabitants exchanged turquoise and other stones for the bright feathers of tropical birds. When they reached Culiacán, their reports mingled with existing legends and convinced an ambitious Spanish viceroy, Antonio de Mendoza, to sponsor a small exploratory expedition northeast toward the pueblos of present-day New Mexico. In 1539, guided by one of the two shipwreck survivors, a black African named Esteban, the expeditionary party set forth. When Esteban, who had gone on ahead, sent back word that he had found seven opulent cities in a land called Cíbola, he gave credence to an elaborate combination of legend, reality, and wishful thinking.

In fact, he had found Zuni, a pueblo in western New Mexico that encompassed a central village and several outlying farming villages. That there were probably only six cities, not seven, and that they were beautiful but not, by Spanish standards, wealthy, the Spanish discovered only later. But at that moment in 1539 the pueblo of Zuni crossed from prehistory to history and entered the ethnocentric written record that served Europeans as a benchmark of civilization. Still the center of their own complex story of themselves, the Zunis were now also peripheral characters in a story of others.[2]

Zuni is just one of many pueblos in New Mexico and Arizona. The most famous, Taos, is north of Santa Fe, and others lie along the banks of the Rio Grande, stretching south from Santa Fe toward Albuquerque. The Hopi pueblos are much farther west, near the Grand Canyon, in Arizona; their reservation today lies within the larger Navajo reservation in that state. Zuni itself is relatively isolated; it lies in a broad, flat valley in New Mexico, close to the Arizona border, surrounded by mountains and divided from its eastern neighbors by both distance and badlands, the remains of a long-inactive volcano.

Like their neighbors, the Zunis trace their ancestry to the builders of the remarkable ruins that still exist in the Southwest, cliff dwellings high in canyon walls and on rock ledges, small cities in valleys like Chaco Canyon and Canyon de Chelly, or on mesa tops, like Mesa Verde. Those settlements flourished in the tenth, eleventh, and twelfth centuries, trading, in some cases, with people as far south as Mexico. By the thirteenth century the people had mysteriously disappeared, the victims of drought or warfare, perhaps, leaving behind these tantalizing traces of their existence. They themselves scattered, in all likelihood, finding their way to other people who took them in, and eventually to the sites of the pueblos that exist today.

No one knows exactly when Zuni was settled, but it was well established when the Spanish arrived in 1539 and began their conquest. The walls of the present pueblo were built at the end of the seventeenth century, on the site of other walls that date much further back. In 1680, the Zunis joined their pueblo neighbors in an uprising against the Spanish. The uprising took the Spanish by surprise, and they retreated temporarily; in 1692 they returned, however, reasserting their authority with acts of legendary brutality, though the Zunis fared somewhat better than the inhabitants of some of the other pueblos. The Zunis, following long-standing tradition, moved into the mountains during the Pueblo Uprising, inhabiting easily defensible caves in the cliffs. When they returned, they rebuilt their town where it is today, consolidating a number of smaller villages into the central pueblo. The pueblo was built of flat stone and adobe, redder and rougher than the golden adobe of Taos; tall outer walls protected the Zunis from intruders, and the ground immediately outside the walls was covered with low-walled gardens, laid out in a waffle pattern designed to maximize the usefulness of the unpredictable rainfall in the valley. Corn, beans, melons, and even peaches grew in this unlikely terrain. Inside, dwellings were stacked one on top of another, with entrances, equipped with ladders, in the roofs. Wonderful chimneys made of stacks of spherical pots dotted the roofs as well, and fruits and vegetables and animal skins were laid out there to dry.

The dwellings were built around central courtyards, and narrow alleys allowed passage through the town. The courtyards and the alleys were the main site of the pueblo's ceremonial dances, though many of them began outside the pueblo. Also vital to Zuni's rituals were kivas, rooms within the pueblo where members of Zuni's secret societies held meetings, performed rituals, and prepared for their roles in the dances. In general, each society was organized around a particular spiritual task, related to healing a specific sort of malady or taking responsibility for some aspect of the pueblo's well-being—helping to bring rain or ensuring a prosperous hunt, for example. Often membership in a medicine society was extended to those whom the society had cured. Adult Zunis belonged to societies that mixed members of many households, in part as a defense against family feuds. For the most part, societies were responsible for discrete parts of Zuni's religious rituals and obligations. Overseeing all of them were six rain priests, who were responsible for making sure that Zuni properly carried out its spiritual obligations, and who, for all intents and purposes, governed the pueblo; they were assisted by the priests of the bow, the warrior society, who put their decisions into practice, shielding the rain priests from the violence and disharmony that might interfere with their spiritual powers. There was also a civil governor, whose job was to deal with outside authorities, first the Spanish, then the Americans.[3]

Each society performed both its own private rituals and public dances, sometimes as part of the yearly dance calendar, sometimes because of particular situations that demanded its intervention. For the public dances, members (most of whom were men) wore costumes that were specific to their societies; these included both special clothing and paint, rattles and other noise-makers, and oversize sculpted masks that identified those who wore them with characters in Zuni's cosmology. Dressed in kachina costumes, the men were representatives of gods and other sacred figures; the kachina dolls that are popular tourist souvenirs today were, in Zuni, made to help children learn the identities of the dancing figures in the courtyards. For those outside Zuni, the most easily identifiable characters in the dances were the Koyemshi and the Newe:kwe, both ritual clowns, though with different responsibilities, and the giant warrior birds, the Sha'lako, whose impersonators wrapped blankets around their shoulders in a way that increased their height by several feet and placed enormous beaked masks atop them. The Sha'lako festival came in the fall, a celebration of the gifts bestowed by the gods and of prayers for continued rains and prosperity.

For two centuries after the Zunis returned to their pueblo following the Pueblo Uprising, their lives consisted of a yearly cycle of farming, herding, and hunting, overlaid by the cycle of their religious obligations. Spanish friars maintained a presence in the pueblo, and the Zunis felt, from time to time, the political and economic demands of the Spanish empire. It is, in fact, important that Zuni was conquered long before there was a United States; it became part of the nation through acquisition, as part of the settlement of the Mexican War in 1848. By then, Zuni, like the other pueblos, had a claim to its land that had legal bearing in Spain, and thus the Zunis existed in a relationship to the United States different from that of other Native American tribes who held their land by tradition but had no formal legal title to it.

Zuni was incorporated into the United States not so much by conquerors as by collectors. There were sporadic visits to the pueblo by curious military men and travelers in the nineteenth century, but it was not until 1879, while the last of the Indian wars were under way, that Americans showed concerted interest in the people who inhabited it. In that year, representatives of the Bureau of American Ethnology made Zuni the focus of the first federally funded experiment in professional anthropology. These representatives initiated a steady flow of anthropologists who were eager to document Zuni's cultural practices and procure extensive collections of its material culture. That flow lasted well into the twentieth century and seems likely to extend into the twenty-first.

Though anthropological interest in Zuni has remained more or less constant since those first encounters, and the pueblo is a well-established stop on the southwestern tourist circuit, neither the Zunis nor those who have studied them are as famous now as they once were. Some of the later students of Zuni, notably Ruth Benedict, Ruth Bunzel, Leslie Spier, Alfred Kroeber, and Elsie Clews Parsons, figure in the history of American anthropology, but few of them are well known to the general public. The individuals who preceded them, including the subjects of this book, are even more obscure. Matilda Stevenson, Frank Hamilton Cushing, and Stewart Culin are relegated to footnotes in the history of anthropology. Yet they have recently begun to attract the attention of people, like myself, who are interested in what the form and substance of their lives and studies reveal about the thinking of Americans of their time.

Stevenson, Cushing, and Culin are now on the margins of the history of anthropology and, in many ways, at the edges of American history. Yet few of us who have explored Indian exhibits in the dark halls of a hundred museums have not brushed up against them. They were part of a small network of people who in a very brief time collected thousands of Native American artifacts. The provenance of some of those pieces was suspicious, and some have recently been repatriated to their rightful owners, but others remain at the heart of exhibits, old and new, that still fascinate children and adults alike. Not everyone has heard of Zuni, and the three anthropologists who first gave shape to our thinking about the pueblo are not world-historical characters. It is not the centrality of Zuni and Zuni anthropology that is compelling but their persistence. Borrowings from Zuni continue to run like a subtle thread woven at the edge of a larger pattern of culture.

Those borrowings from Zuni, in the form of anthropological works, run as well through the identities Matilda Stevenson, Frank Hamilton Cushing, and Stewart Culin crafted for themselves. As they developed those identities, they also contributed to defining the new discipline of anthropology and its distinguishing methodology: fieldwork. Like other anthropologists working with other Native American societies, they constructed portraits of the cultures they studied that reached an extraordinary number of people: readers of popular magazines, visitors to museums, and the crowds that swept through the grounds of the world's fairs regularly offering up science, spectacle, and amusement at the turn of the century.

Within those portraits, and within the biographies of these three anthropologists, we can discern a complicated dialogue that touched on many issues that concerned Americans as the nineteenth century gave way to the twentieth. The center of this book is Zuni, but it is also a study in the cultural history of the urban United States, an attempt to shed light on the simultaneous feelings of confidence and upheaval that some middle-class Americans experienced when they sought to accommodate the new economic and social realities of a maturing national marketplace, new bureaucratic organizations, and new ideas about leisure, personal fulfillment, and identity. As corporate culture and the culture of consumption started to exert their powerful influences, Americans' understanding of their own identities changed.[4]

Zuni pueblo served, not entirely voluntarily, as a laboratory for a generation of anthropologists who were defining a new profession and documenting the particulars of pre-industrial society. Over several decades, they produced an extraordinary body of literature on Zuni and collected thousands of Zuni artifacts. To the extent that a society's culture can be preserved in these alienated forms, Stevenson, Cushing, and Culin did a remarkable job. But their Zuni, necessarily frozen in time and removed in space, exists in a strange relation to the Zuni of New Mexico today. For while urban American anthropologists assembled the culture in one time and space, Zuni perpetuated itself in another. The culture that the anthropologists re-created looked a lot like Zuni, but both the means and the ends of their endeavor existed not in New Mexico but in the cities of modern America.

For anthropologists, Zuni was a gold mine of artifacts and information, with an abundance of materials from which ideas about its culture and about culture in general could be inferred. Zuni, only one of many societies of indigenous Americans subjected to scrutiny at the turn of the century, was an intriguing and accessible research site. The pueblo provided the material and cultural subject matter that turn-of-the-century anthropologists so avidly sought, and that they then transported and transformed for professional study and popular consumption. But Zuni served both the anthropologists and their audiences in less tangible ways, supplying these inhabitants of an industrial world with a stage set against which they could play out their fantasies of pre-industrial wholeness and cultural superiority. Within the stone and adobe walls of Zuni, anthropologists pursued their individual quests for identity and purpose. When they shipped back Zuni artifacts and set up exhibits, and when they brought Zuni people east, they offered up for comparison a new rendering of American social identity. Here was a way to make peace with the tantalizing and troubling realities of an industrial consumer society. What the Zunis really were, what their culture meant, was of secondary importance. The Zunis, as a part of American popular culture, were more important for being what other Americans wanted them to be than for what they actually were.

Stevenson, Cushing, and Culin presented much of the physical and cultural material they collected at Zuni in exhibits and writings. Because they arrived at the pueblo so early, and because they acquired so many artifacts and so much firsthand information as yet largely protected from outside influences, they laid the groundwork for the imaginative uses that many other people have made of Zuni. Anthropologists, artists and writers, and visitors to museums and world's fairs were all fascinated by the possibility of traveling in another time and space and experiencing another way of ordering the universe. These three made their own creative uses of Zuni, contributing early chapters in the story of how Zuni came to occupy its position as an island refuge at the edge of the American imagination.

Zuni's history since the arrival of the Spanish, and especially since the arrival of Americans more than three centuries later, had about it an air of romance and fantasy; it had entered the larger historical record as both a place and an idea, and so it remained. The magic of the myth of the Seven Cities of Cíbola never wholly wore off, and to this was added the nostalgia of many visitors to Zuni for the pre-industrial past and the vibrant spirituality that it seemed to represent. By the end of the nineteenth century, when Zuni was invaded not by conquistadores but by anthropologists, it was imagined as an island away from the tempest of modern life, a place where the demands of modern civilization were temporarily suspended and the harsh experience of savagery tempered civilization's metal. It offered visitors from the industrializing United States a world turned upside down, separated from the real world not in time but in space. It was a place away from the rules of everyday life, a respite from the obligations of the city.

But it was also a place for science, for without their scientific purposes, the travels of Stevenson, Cushing, and Culin would have lost their moral weight. Sampling the practices of primitive life brought them dangerously close to scandal; such proximity to excess could be justified only by devotion to a scientific calling. In the case of these anthropologists, the work of Zuni was in part a mission of preservation—rescuing a culture they believed would not long survive. It was also part of a larger project aimed at filling in the details of a universal story of human cultural evolution, a scientific creation story in the making. This first generation of anthropologists believed that studying so-called primitive cultures in places like Zuni would in time reveal a pattern of cul-

tural evolution that would give coherence to the perplexing pro-
fusion of variations on culture that people of European ancestry
encountered as they spread their imperial reaches farther and
farther afield.

Carrying this scientific creation story, as well as the more familiar Christian one that framed it, these anthropologists ventured forth to find out how they could fit other societies into
their narratives. Because their quarry was culture, a central part
of their work was the investigation of native creation stories, part
of the oral traditions that were the most fragile and elusive of anthropological artifacts. At Zuni, their urge to find a scientific explanation for the varieties of mankind mixed with their study of
sacred traditions in a manner that generated an irresistible challenge and a wonderful, if troubling, synthesis. The stories were
among the hardest things to obtain, as sacred things generally
are. And because they were works of art, magical, mystical, and
beautiful as well as scientific, these stories exerted a peculiar
charm over these Americans, who simultaneously dismissed
mysticism as primitive and embraced it with a powerful nostalgia. More than that, they represented, to the discerning eye of
Frank Hamilton Cushing, a sort of Rosetta Stone that contained
not only the spiritual heart of Zuni culture but coded clues to its
prehistoric past as well.

When anthropologists came to Zuni, four versions of creation
converged. There was the Zuni mythology of the origins of the
pueblo; a version of it that Cushing created out of a combination
of archaeology, careful reading, and imagination; the Christian
beliefs of the Anglo-American visitors; and the larger scientific
narrative that, they hoped, would unite all the others. This last
meta-narrative was to be the story of the evolution of cultures, a
story that encompassed all other stories, weaving together the
strands of all existing societies into a grand teleological narrative
that had Anglo-Saxon culture as its final chapter.

One theme that recurs in the work of historians, anthropologists, and other writers on Zuni concerns the way the Zunis managed to absorb cultural forms from outside without perceptibly altering their own core beliefs and practices. The Spanish friars who followed the conquistadores built a mission in the pueblo early in the seventeenth century but could not convince the Zunis to give up their own religious traditions and rituals. The Zunis adopted some Christian practices but could not see Christianity and their own pantheon of gods as mutually exclusive. Centuries later, Mormon and Presbyterian missionaries encountered the same stubborn confidence. Though they were adept at incorporating useful ideas into their existing practices, the Zunis remained convinced that abandoning their obligations to their own spiritual world would be disastrous. The anthropologists who followed these earlier religious envoys noted with bemusement and frustration that the Zunis seemed determined to impose their own meanings on the trappings of Western, Christian society that came to the pueblo, diminishing its usefulness as a "pure" example of primitive life without noticeably advancing the cause of the civilization those trappings represented. In their ethnocentric confidence that their own gods were ultimately the most powerful, the Zunis were more like their American visitors than those visitors were able to see.

The fact is, Zunis had imagined themselves for centuries before they were imagined by Europeans and Americans. Their own story, the cultural narrative that explains who they are and what they should do, is the story of a journey, the journey to the Middle Place. Like the stories of some of their southwestern neighbors, the Zuni story begins in a series of four underground chambers. These chambers contain creatures who are not yet finished humans. Some have tails, some webbed hands and feet; all live in darkness or semidarkness. Some of those from the uppermost chambers have come out into the light, but they offend the Sun by neglecting the necessary rituals, and so the smell of each succeeding group has killed off those who reached the surface before them. Finally, the Sun, anxious that the last group, in the deepest chamber, emerge in the right way, creates twin sons out of foam and sends them to show the people the way out.

The way is arduous. The Ahayuuta, the twin sons, must figure out, with the help of the people, how to get out of the darkness. They consult the priests of each direction, and gather them together, each with his own knowledge, power, and sacred objects. In time, they develop a plan that involves creating trees that grow from each level up to the next. As each tree reaches through to the next room, the people climb up until finally they reach the surface of the earth.

Once there, they embark on a journey across the land. This creation story reverses the expulsion of Adam and Eve that marks the beginning of a journey in Jewish and Christian mythology, and the difference reflects a basic difference between the two cultures. Whereas Judeo-Christianity begins with expulsion, followed by generations of restless wandering in hopes of recapturing an original place and state of being, the Zuni religion begins with a journey from an unlovely place that ends in the place the Zunis are meant to be, the Middle Place. The story of that journey is wonderfully rich, and I would do it an injustice by trying to summarize it all here. It is a journey full of tests and trials. The people don't always understand what they are supposed to do, and, like the descendants of Adam and Eve, they accumulate the burdens of humanity and history along the way. They meet other creatures, supernatural and natural, who influence the progress of their quest, and they themselves split up, some traveling in one direction, some in another, for it is not clear exactly where it is they are headed. When some of them reach the area around Zuni, they begin to build villages and settle down, but the Ahayuuta continue to search for the Middle Place. After a long time, they come to Zuni. Summoning the water-strider, a delicate creature that can run on the surface of water, they ask him to spread out his long arms and legs, and they mark the place where his heart rests. This, finally, is the Middle Place. This is Zuni.[5]

The emphasis on place is crucial in the spiritual world of Zuni, both to the Zunis and to the Americans who longed for such a sense of place. The Zunis' sense of ownership of the landscape around them fascinated anthropologists. It was not exactly the idea of private property deified in the world of capitalist accumulation; rather, the Zunis had a clear sense of which parts of which land other people might use only with their permission. They understood that some property, land, and goods belonged to individuals, but not all of those things could be bought and sold, as they could in the world of capital. For example, each of the elaborate masks used in the ceremonial dances at Zuni was the possession of an individual and a family, and they were responsible for its care and keeping. But what was owned here was a social responsibility, not the object itself. Individual possession shaded imperceptibly into communal ownership. In the same way, the land owned and farmed by individual Zunis shaded into a world of places inhabited by supernatural beings who were active participants in Zuni life. The claims of these beings, and of the community, were more powerful than those of individuals. The boundaries at Zuni were permeable, but everyone knew what they were.

Frank Cushing was probably the first anthropologist to grasp the Zunis' sense of the land. Cushing had his faults, but he was an extraordinarily perceptive and imaginative listener. He spent a good deal of time listening to the Zunis' stories of themselves, as well as exploring the region around Zuni and examining the ruins that, according to Zuni traditions, had been the homes of the Zunis' ancestors. When he wrote up his collection of Zuni creation stories for the Bureau of American Ethnology's annual report for 1891–1892, he prefaced them with a lengthy discourse on Zuni's past. Employing the tools of archaeology and anthropology, Cushing had found what he believed to be a thread of history running through what otherwise seemed to be tales of gods and spirits in a metaphysical realm, products not of history but of the Zunis' collective imagination. How innovative his discovery was is unclear. Certainly the Zunis understood their stories to be both history and something larger. But most Americans had no other experience of Zuni to draw on, so Cushing offered a guide to the Zuni stories, a way for Americans to understand that what the Zunis took to be accounts of intercession by supernatural beings were time-darkened elaborations on age-old stories of migration, conquest, and amalgamation.

Cushing began by asserting that the Zunis were "the earliest known of all the tribes within the territory of the United States." They remained, he wrote, "as regards their social and religious institutions and customs and their modes of thought, if not their daily life, the most archaic of the Pueblo or Aridian peoples. They still continue to be, as they have for centuries been, the most highly developed, yet characteristic and representative of all these people."[6] Whether the Zunis were, in fact, the most archaic, highly developed, characteristic, and representative of all the pueblo peoples is debatable, but in making these claims Cushing was arguing that they might stand in as the progenitors of the region and the proprietors of pueblo religious traditions. If this was so, his story could be the first story, the origin story, of at least this region of the continent, and thus the foundation for that universal story of human cultural evolution that was the goal of his science.

Having established the Zunis as representative of both a very early historical time and a remote region, Cushing guided his readers through the prehistoric landscape of their ancestors. He deduced a dual ancestry for them from his observation of physical types in the pueblo as well as from the existence of "numerous survivals—inherited, not borrowed—of the arts, customs, myths, and institutions of at least two peoples." The narrative he fashioned traced the emergence, in the early part of the second millennium of the common era, of a successful cliff-dwelling culture that spread out into the more spacious plains and mesa tops as its population became more numerous and more secure.[7] To this larger group of ancestors, which he identified as native to the region near Zuni (they were probably Anasazis, from north of Zuni, and perhaps Mogollons from the south), he assigned relative sophistication in architecture and in the "peaceful arts." The "intrusive" branch of the Zuni family tree was essentially transient, by contrast, coming from the area of the Little Colorado River. This branch had a much cruder architecture and standard of living, but also greater physical and spiritual vitality. It was the migratory travels of this second group that figured most prominently in Zuni mythology. This group, Cushing suggested, was related to the Yuma tribes that still existed along the Little Colorado, and was "the one most told of in the myths, the one which speaks throughout them in the first person; that is, which claims to be the original Shiwi or Zuni."[8]

Cushing had detailed reasons for his assumptions: the squaring of the cave dwellers' architectural forms as they evolved out into the plains and met the builders of rectangular wooden houses; the existence of a double set of terms in the Zuni language for important concepts like the directions, with common usages deriving from the aboriginal culture and archaic, ritual names deriving from the original home of the transients; the superimposition of shared dwellings on a system among the cliff dwellers that segregated women and children safely above the men.[9] In this way, too, the mystical beings of Zuni myths were given a rational basis. The Koyemshi, Zuni's ritual clowns, for example, wore strange knob-covered masks that seemed to refer to no particular feature of the desert environment. But, Cushing argued, they did suggest a muddy rock formation that relatives of the Yuma might have known. Oddly incongruous in the south-western desert, the mudheads, as they are sometimes called, made more sense as part of a story of migrants.[10] Likewise, Cushing looked carefully at folk tales in which parents, through death or capture, abandoned the children they had hidden in granaries that were purposefully difficult to get to. The children miraculously survived on the meager food there, and emerged later "as great warrior-magicians and deliver[ed] their captive elders." He compared these tales with archaeological evidence that suggested they had historical foundations. Archaeologists had found the unburied bodies of children in windowless storage chambers in back of the cliff dwellings, apparently left alone by the adults who had put them there to protect them. That Cushing could thus find natural sources for the supernatural imagery in Zuni myths suggested to his readers that the mythology in general might be understood as having been extrapolated from history and geography, rather than being some incomprehensible metaphysical absolute.[11]

In short, Cushing promised rational comprehensibility. Tackling a range of extremely obscure practices with the tools of the linguist and the archaeologist, and with anthropological methods of analogy (the idea that the practices of past societies can be deduced from those of similar living cultures) and re-creation (reproducing artifacts under conditions similar to those experienced by ancient craftspeople), Cushing suggested that, given time and study, all that seemed mysterious and alien in cultures like Zuni's could be decoded rationally, revealing the universal patterns of evolution and migration at their core. He claimed to be able to trace Zuni prehistory in a continuous line back from modern pueblos to early cave dwellers, and he was willing to speculate authoritatively about a period even earlier than that. Like the ancient trail that he followed from the country of the cliff dwellers to the valley of the Zuni Salt Lake, south of Zuni pueblo, where the two ancestral peoples seemed to have met, Cushing read in the landscape, with the help of Zuni mythology, an unbroken history running for hundreds of miles, worn into the landscape over hundreds of years. The landscape itself, with its worn trails and ruined structures, became, then, the text of a history for an unlettered, "prehistorical" people.[12]

It was perceptive of Cushing to recognize that Zuni mythology was more than the exotic tales of an unsophisticated people. He understood that the culture's stories grew up around significant experiences and that, by holding the landscape and the myths together, one could guess at what those experiences had been. Furthermore, he developed a new tool for his survey of Zuni culture that took him well beyond the walls of the pueblo. What he first thought of as the culture of a small contained village unfolded, under his investigations, to reveal an entire region thick with human history. Cushing was eventually able to map not only the sacred sites to which the Zunis guided him (as well as some they wished to keep secret) but also the sites that for the Zunis existed only vaguely in myth.

Cushing, in effect, constructed his own creation story for Zuni, with the story recast as one of science, not of spirit, and he offered it to the readers of the Bureau of American Ethnology's annual report as a preamble to the Zunis' own stories. His version was a double translation of the Zuni tales he had transcribed—translated first from Zuni to English and then from metaphysical to physical. Cushing was not simply an observer; he was using Zuni culture as raw material for his own creations. In his position as an adopted member of the Zuni tribe, he acted out his conviction that he could represent Zuni ancestors, by virtue of the universality of the human mind and his willingness to put his own mind to work within the structural confines of the world of those ancestors who had crafted the culture's mythology. Re-creating the historical circumstances of that spiritual creation, he reconfigured the myths as scientific explanation. In doing so, he presented himself as being of Zuni, yet better at understanding Zuni than the Zunis were themselves. To his other culture, he offered a linear, scientifically framed narrative of the continent's prehistory that fit, in language and in tone, as a preamble to the history of the United States.

Zuni's prehistory connected a people who had lived in the pueblo for centuries with other people who had occupied the continent for even longer. In his introduction to the Zunis' creation stories, Cushing artfully gave the New World a pedigree, a story of human life and art that, if it wasn't as ancient or as glorious as the story of Christian Europe, nevertheless gave a patina of old age to a place many Europeans and even some Americans still viewed as raw and rude. To link that prehistory to the written record of the accomplishments of the United States, the nation that now claimed sovereignty over Zuni, Cushing and the other anthropologists who studied Zuni had the advantage of a fairly comprehensive Spanish historical record that, conveniently, started in the world of myth.

It was through the myth of the Seven Cities of Cíbola that Zuni left the unlettered universe of prehistory and entered Spanish history and the European imagination, and thus entered American history, because in the Southwest, Spanish, not British, history formed the early chapters of the American story. Zuni was officially annexed to the Spanish empire when, in 1540, an army led by Francisco Vásquez de Coronado retraced the steps of the 1539 expedition and conquered Cíbola's inhabitants. The Zuni people, occupants of six small farming villages, were forced at point of lance and gun into the stream of a larger historical narrative. The history of Spanish America includes the attempts by Spanish friars over the next century and a half to convert the

Zunis to Catholicism; the successful Pueblo Uprising that briefly drove out the Spanish in 1680 and the reconquest that followed; the waning of Spanish, then Mexican, interest; and the incorporation of the territory that encompassed the pueblo into the United States at the end of the Mexican War in 1848.

In 1869, eight years before he published *Ancient Society*, his influential treatise on social evolution, Lewis Henry Morgan tackled what he considered to be the still unsolved problem of the Seven Cities of Cíbola in an article in *The North American Review*. This article, which held the seeds of the reasoning that governs his famous book, was a review essay. Morgan pored over nine different accounts of travels in the Southwest, six of which concerned the Spanish expeditions of 1539 and 1540, looking for evidence their writers had missed about the location of these majestic cities. Convinced (though later archaeologists were not) that Zuni was not Cíbola, Morgan nevertheless believed that seven real cities had inspired the myth, and that a careful reading of the archaeological record would, in time, locate them. On the basis of the Spanish written record, he could come up only with the hypothesis that the Seven Cities of Cíbola would be found somewhere in the region of Chaco Canyon. In the process of expounding this misguided thesis, however, he rehearsed the Spanish history of the Zuni region, providing anthropologists with a digest of the early European observations of its people. This record of other encounters with Zuni allowed those anthropologists to approach the pueblo with a sense of its place in recent history.

Zuni was subjected to the generalizing tendencies that afflicted most early anthropologists in their search for evidence of a universal pattern of social evolution. Both the extensiveness of its historical record and the uniqueness of its culture made it a rich subject of study and a fascinating place. Morgan's review of the Spanish histories of the region allowed early students familiarity with the culture even if they did not understand the Zuni language and its oral traditions. The work of Cushing and Matilda Stevenson, coming early, when much that was later destroyed or altered was still intact, laid the groundwork for those who followed, including Stewart Culin, who came to Zuni as much to memorialize Cushing as to study Zuni.

Zuni was special. Other tribes shared linguistic genealogies, but the Zuni language has no direct relatives elsewhere in the Americas. Removed from both the cluster of pueblos along the Rio Grande to the east and the mesa villages of the Hopi to the west, all of Zuni society was contained in the single pueblo and its outlying villages, which were occupied only during the farming season. With its reputation for stubbornly ignoring or suborning the influence of Spanish culture and for its strong, dramatic dance traditions, Zuni was a perfect society for anthropologists to study. In turn, it offers a perfect context in which to study those anthropologists.

Two

IMAGINING AMERICA

———✧✧✧———

In a report to Bureau of American Ethnology administrators in 1883, the fourth year of his stay with the Zunis, Frank Cushing recounted an adventure that he had had in the Hopi pueblo of Oraibi, a hundred miles or so northwest of Zuni and about halfway to the Grand Canyon. To the people of Oraibi, assembled in a kiva usually used for ceremonial purposes, he gave a remarkable performance. Intending to persuade the Oraibis to give him artifacts for the National Museum in Washington, Cushing commanded the reluctant audience to listen as he conjured up a vision. "Among the many great Houses in the Pueblo of Washington," he told them, "is one of red and blue stone, with great roofs and terraces, and a dome so high that the strongest hand cannot throw a stone over it. This dome is filled with plates like quartz-crystals, that the light may shine in, and even the sun-rays themselves may enter." In that enormous house, there were many rooms, he said, "for there are stored in boxes one can see through, the fabrications of the many different children of Washington."

The purpose of these rooms full of boxes was genealogical:

Washington's "chiefs," including Cushing, wanted to determine whether Washington's children—the Native Americans—were related to one another (and by extension to white Americans). But, he continued, getting to the point, one of the rooms in this splendid house was sadly empty: the room reserved for the Oraibis. Cushing had come to the pueblo to fill this last room and to complete the American genealogy. "Washington has sent me to you with my brothers," he told the Oraibis, "that we may get things wherewith to fill this room. That we may put them in the boxes one can look into when closed, to keep them for many years."[1]

The National Museum was then housed in the Arts and Industries building, which still stands next door to the Smithsonian Castle on the Mall in Washington. In 1879, when Cushing left that city for the Southwest, you could still board the train on the Mall, which was less impressive than it is today; the Washington Monument, construction of which was interrupted by the Civil War, was not yet complete, and most of the other memorials that now grace that vast public space lay in the future. But the Arts and Industries building, which had been constructed primarily to house exhibits from the Philadelphia Centennial Exposition of 1876, was a sign of things to come.

The phrasing of Cushing's appeal to the Oraibis has the familiar ring of speeches in which imperial white men translate concepts from industrialized society into pre-industrial terms. He wanted to impress the Oraibis by equating and comparing the National Museum with the pueblos that structured their own lives. He offered them inclusion in the national family, symbolized by the museum, as well as more concrete benefits—clothing, food, and tools—if they agreed to supply him with the artifacts of their culture.

But the real audience for Cushing's impassioned presentation resided in the Pueblo of Washington. It was the administration of the Bureau of American Ethnology, the body responsible for funding his work. The concepts he translated for the Oraibis were second nature to denizens of the Smithsonian. In re-creating the drama for fellow scientists, with simplified, Indian-ized phrases, he highlighted the amusing contrast between primitive and scientific knowledge, while simultaneously claim-ing for the latter all the mystery and romance he had found in southwestern Indian culture. Moreover, in this short recitation, Cushing affirmed his era's faith in the power of objects, a faith that matched that of the people he meant to disposses of every-thing from gods to sandals.

Frank Cushing and his colleagues, Matilda Stevenson and Stewart Culin, who also scoured the Southwest for artifacts at the turn of the century, were anthropologist-curators. They moved between Native American villages, museums, professional meet-ings, and popular expositions, and as they did so they created not only a new discipline but a new and popular visual language, a vocabulary of signs and symbols accessible to people across the social spectrum. Anthropology exhibits were designed by people whose interests and understandings may have been esoteric, but their ubiquitous presence among popular amusements at the turn of the century made them part of the common language of American culture.

Museums, and by extension the exhibition halls their cura-tors helped to fill at world's fairs, taught as much through their physical structure as they did through the objects they displayed. Their monumental design, which usually featured high ceilings and, in the days before good artificial lighting, magnificent win-dows, linked them with cathedrals and churches as places of rev-erence and awe, as did the apparent comprehensiveness of the exhibits. The claims to scientific authority made by natural-history museums—just the facts—separated them from earlier cabinets of curiosities like Barnum's Museum, even though what they exhibited often rivaled two-headed chickens as objects of wonder and amusement. Their focus on things that were laid out enticingly in glass cases linked them to the cities' new department stores, palaces of the vigorous new forms of consumer culture then taking shape. For turn-of-the-century anthropologists, objects spoke with a reassuring stability. Once they had laid out their artifacts in polished wood-and-glass cases along carefully ordered axes, they were confident that they had done what was necessary to reveal the meaning of those artifacts. Like the massive buildings that housed them, the exhibits were solid and the perspective was fixed, giving curators and visitors alike a sense that here meanings were solidly reliable. None of these structural messages were accidental, and all of them contributed to making museums three-dimensional illustrations of the prehistory of the nation.[2]

Museums were the primary site of serious professional anthropology between 1880 and 1920, but they were also the production site for very popular entertainment. The conflict between these two functions intensified after 1900, as the discipline moved slowly but surely out of the museum and into the university. But in the early decades no such division was possible: professional and popular aims were joined, and each influenced the other. The museums in which anthropologists became curators were dynamic public spaces, and the exhibits were meant to mediate between the elite world of the scientists and the public they depended on to support their work. As visitors stood in front of the glass display cases, as they looked at models of villages or contemplated costumed figures isolated on shelves or grouped in vignettes from everyday life, a dialogue took place without anyone's uttering a word. And that dialogue was concerned far more with the figures reflected in the glass, in the act of peering in, than with the frozen figures and missing subjects of the objects within.

The dialogue touched on all the crucial issues of the day. The buildings, with their neat rows of display cases, were monuments to the period's search for order. In their halls, everything was classified, and latent natural and social hierarchies were made manifest. There, visitors looked at exhibits whose content raised the subject of the dispossession of Native Americans. Could a nation that seemed to be driving indigenous peoples to the brink of extinction maintain its sense of mission and destiny? Could Washington really bring all its children into a single house, into the nation? Who *were* the children of Washington represented here—captive, in the inert artifacts behind glass—and what was their relationship to the children who stood outside looking in? Did they bear a message that could ease the longings of a people nostalgic for their own past?

Anthropologists had to find answers for these questions, and their answers had both private and political ramifications. Their exhibits invited viewers to join the discussion and to contemplate these troubling issues. But in the end, in the fatalistic combination of evolution and progress and in the reassuring bittersweetness of nostalgia, they offered moral justification for the acts of the nation and for their own complicity in the final dispossession of the Indians. The discussion was open to anyone who came to the museum, because, despite the esoteric nature of the science and the complexity of the moral questions, the exhibits spoke a comfortable common language. Their images seemed familiar, even if the objects themselves were exotic. Cabinets of curiosities, freak shows, Barnumesque museums, and Victorian knickknack shelves all prepared museumgoers for the displays they found. Moreover, curators borrowed the display techniques of department stores and the artistry of amusement parks and reiterated their values.

But the museums framed their images scientifically, transforming voyeuristic, entertaining, and frivolous motives into something worthy of the reverence inspired by their cathedral ceilings and hushed halls. The claims of science were everywhere visible in the ordered presentation and in the neat labels, and they were implicit in the surgical process that had removed the objects from their human, cultural context. Anthropologist-curators encouraged viewers to position themselves in a world of things, a world that represented the larger, messier human world but was contained, safe, and comprehensible. They offered a paradigm for looking at others, accounting for the distanced view and inequalities of power by casting the act of looking as one of scientific observation, subject to a special set of ethics. In this environment, museumgoers were invited to compare their own civilization with those of the makers of the artifacts on display. That comparison was heavily weighted in favor of the industrial society that built the museum, and it made conquest seem both natural—part of the evolution of cultures—and moral.

Exhibits of artifacts enabled visitors to take possession of the intimate details of a passing way of life. And these sympathetic individual acts helped to blunt the edges of the larger, bloodier social acts by which Americans had taken possession of Indian land. Anthropologists and the exhibits they mounted helped to make that possession spiritual as well as physical, extending to the conquerors not only the land but the natives' rootedness in it. Gazing at the apparently straightforward visual images fixed in glass cases in museum halls, Americans could reconcile their democratic ideals with their otherwise dissonant cultural yearnings for Indian land and for a spiritual sense of connectedness with the American landscape. This was possible precisely because the museums' "science" encompassed the exotic, mystical, dangerous, and romantic elements that derived from anthropology's essential connection with the world of popular amusements.

To the extent that Frank Cushing, Matilda Stevenson, and Stewart Culin pieced together their lives out of available materials, they were just like anyone else, but chance and inclination conspired to make remarkably interesting materials available to them. History has so far noted primarily their idiosyncracies: Cushing's flamboyant play with Indian forms and his imaginative reconstructions; Stevenson's self-centered myopia as she struggled with the obstacles that her own culture threw in her path because she was a woman; Culin's focus on material artifacts to the virtual exclusion of the people who made them; and a marked lack of humor and irony among them all. Yet, in their own time, the three anthropologists successfully and creatively exploited both access to the Zunis and the yet imperfectly defined parameters of their science, and they became interesting and important in a society in which other people of their class were experiencing diminished autonomy and authority. They thought of themselves as central, not peripheral, to the development of anthropology, and other people regarded them in that light as well. Moreover, they understood themselves to be part of a project that was of national importance: the preservation of the material and intellectual legacy of the continent's threatened indigenous peoples. These three idiosyncratic characters are interesting representatives of an extraordinary time in the United States, and in the dissonance between their stories and the biographies of more conventional figures of the period, they raise important questions about the tensions and opportunities within American culture in their own time as well as today.

The Progressive movement no longer suffices to sum up the immensely complex, very fluid nature of American culture during the turn of the last century. But part of its legacy to historians seems to have been the sense of movement at the core of contemporary Americans' idea of progress. The years from 1877 to 1920 were far more than a bridge between two centuries, though efforts to characterize them fasten on the idea of transition, with both its promise of change and its sense of loss.[3] These years witnessed the birth of modernity, an extremely problematic, constantly shifting concept that encompassed the coming of age of industrial capitalism and the profound cultural changes that it occasioned: urbanization; a new industrial work culture, both on the factory floor and in management; a new form of professionalism and new sources of identity for the middle class; an increasingly continental context for activities that had once been understood locally; the development of an economy directed at individual consumers and, consequently, a culture in which consumption became a way of thinking as well as a form of economic interaction.

The thousands of smaller changes that made up these seismic shifts created, like a pointillist painting, a vision of the world that was perceptible only from a distance. The age was marked by the emergence of extraordinary unifying forces, hallmarks of expanding industrial capitalism that included, importantly, the vertical integration of businesses and transcontinental railroads. But along with these forces of incorporation Americans experienced fragmentation and alienation, extensive social dislocation, and disturbing labor unrest. An awareness of these other forces underlay the intellectual crisis that historians have identified during this period, and they were part of the reason for the reform movements that proliferated as the United States remade itself as a continental economy and a modern centralized state. The prevalence of reform and reformers among a significant group of influential Americans attests to their essentially optimistic outlook. The reorienting of American culture at this time had its roots in fears of disintegration and loss, but it expressed itself eloquently in forms of mastery. Like modern painters who struggled to find a way to represent a multiplicity of perspectives on two-dimensional canvases, a new class of American professionals recognized the fragmentation of their intellectual universe but were confident that those fragments could still be assembled into something meaningful and whole.[4]

It was anthropology's contribution to offer a way to set the fragments of various cultures into whole understandings, to harness the past to the present and the future. A newly professionalized science specifically devoted to old things, it had an intellectual paradigm that offered a strategy for straddling the quintessential divide in modernism: an enthusiasm for progress perpetually shadowed by a nostalgia for what progress had destroyed. In the new discipline's very nature was the idea that the two could coexist, that the past was an integral part of the present, that the narrative of human history could spell out the connections between the two. With that narrative and with the objects in which it was written came, as well, the promise of ownership, of belonging to a continent that didn't yet feel quite like home.

The generation in search of order was the generation that shaped anthropology in its early days. This was the generation that the historian Burton Bledstein has labeled the mid-Victorians. Having come of age intellectually in the 1860s and 1870s, somewhat earlier than the Progressives, they had many Progressive traits, but their outlook and expectations were still fundamentally nineteenth-century. Frank Cushing, Matilda Stevenson, and Stewart Culin were near-perfect mid-Victorians. They were rather average middle-class people who found in the fluidity of the years after the Civil War a chance to be extraordinary. They craved respectability and prestige, they liked to be in control of the situation, and they were fascinated by the exotic and the remote. Matilda Stevenson seems to have been most concerned with appearing respectable, perhaps because, as a woman, her brushes with the primitive and her aspirations to professionalism put her respectability most in question. Frank Cushing affected a dispassionate professionalism, but he craved recognition for his work. Stewart Culin was an excellent example of a certain kind of mid-Victorian adventurer: he loved to explore unusual places, like the Chinese quarter of Philadelphia or the

Zuni pueblo, and to return with wonderful things. In new technologies and institutional structures that, as they matured, were to define the twentieth century, these three people found ways to satisfy their nineteenth-century cravings. Railroads allowed them to indulge, with Huck Finn, the desire to light out for the territories quite literally, and anthropology permitted them not only to carry their respectability with them but to enhance it as they went.

Anthropology was not a new science in the 1890s. The history of anthropological thought in the United States reaches back at least as far as Thomas Jefferson's *Notes on the State of Virginia*, and Stevenson, Cushing, and Culin belong to a rich and often troubling American tradition that developed in the early nineteenth century. Before the Civil War, such thinking provided the underpinnings for a defense of slavery on the grounds that Africans were a biologically inferior, even decadent race. After that, it coalesced, still deeply marked by racism, in the work of more progressive thinkers, including Lewis Henry Morgan. But the urgent intention to salvage native cultures that characterized the discipline when it began to professionalize at the end of the century was also closely related to trends in business, government, and reform to develop abstract models or systems that would organize and direct all sorts of human behavior: Frederick W. Taylor designed systems to break down the arts and crafts of skilled workers into measured movements that they could do interchangeably; Melvil Dewey devised a systematic classification of all the categories of human knowledge, heretofore and to come, for libraries; and Lewis Henry Morgan thought that he discerned a universal pattern of human cultural evolution. Sciences and social sciences adopted this devotion to system and classification from the well-ordered businesses around them, claiming both efficiency and order, two watchwords of the period. The possibilities for a systematic study of mankind's precursors seemed limitless, and were multiplied exponentially by the capacities of new technologies, especially the rail lines that extended deep into the heart of the Indian Territory. Those railroads transformed the amateur collector on horseback into the scientific ethnologist able to come and go almost at will, to stay connected to his or her own culture while living among other peoples, and to ship back not just traces of other cultures but comprehensive chunks of them, enough to re-create them somewhere else for study in years to come.

The changes in intellectual milieu that would, in time, inspire Franz Boas and his followers to establish a truly professional anthropology in American universities had already begun, but most practitioners, including Boas himself, were still using older methodologies. The hallmarks of this age in anthropology were systematic study and the creation of compendiums of cultural information; the emphasis was on preservation—salvage— far more than on interpretation. The institutional center of much of this early work was the Bureau of American Ethnology, which was founded in 1879 as part of the bill that created the U.S. Geological Survey out of a series of competing western surveys that aimed at mapping the resources of the country in the years after the Civil War. It was headed, as was the Geological Survey, by John Wesley Powell, who put both his political and his intellectual talents to work on behalf of this mission to document Native American history and culture.

In their work at Zuni and elsewhere among Native Americans, Cushing, Stevenson, and Culin helped to establish a tenuous link with the new century. Like Mark Twain's Connecticut Yankee, they could gain a certain power in an older social structure by exploiting more modern understandings, languages, and inventions. They did this at Zuni, treating minor illnesses with modern medicines, mysteriously producing India ink when the Zunis desperately needed it for ceremonial purposes, trading sleigh bells and shells from far away for Zuni artifacts and information. But they also did it in Washington, New York, and Boston, dazzling people there with both their exhibits of primitive and exotic material, and their explanations of it. When Matilda Stevenson invited Washington dignitaries to her reception for the Zuni "princess" We'wha in 1885, they came to see a scientist and her subject, not a mere curiosity. Stewart Culin used the railroad to cross time and space so that he could bring back an extraordinary artifactual reproduction of mysterious Zuni practices. And Frank Cushing, who might, with Stevenson, have been considered a crank or an eccentric in an earlier period, was received by Boston society in all seriousness as a representative both of Zuni and of science because he could speak both their languages.[5]

Not yet bound by the rigid empirical standards of a university discipline or by the requirements of a degree or a certificate, these three individuals were nonetheless professionals in a new sense, and could present their work not as a hobby but as a science. To use the metaphor that shaped much of their consciousness, they were part of an evolutionary dead end, a branch that connected the new with the old but would itself die out. In the trials and errors that marked their careers, we see them developing practices that shaped their discipline. More than that, though, because of anthropology's peculiar subject matter and geographic arena, their work sheds light on questions that are of significance to the nation as a whole. Cushing and Stevenson in particular, as members of the first Bureau of American Ethnology field expedition, adopted and adapted scientific approaches to the collection of artifacts and information on-site, and they contributed both positive and negative examples to the new practice of fieldwork that united the history of anthropology with the cultural history of America. Anthropological fieldwork offered Americans an important way to possess not only Native American artifacts but Native American culture and history, and even the Native American claim to the land. Fused to the evolutionary assumptions of anthropology, fieldwork underwrote stories that made dispossession seem right and natural.

When the Spanish arrived at Zuni, they were already imagining the Seven Cities of Cíbola. So, too, the first anthropologists to reach the pueblo had a story in mind. Though anthropology had long been an amateur pursuit among American intellectuals, many of whom were wrestling with issues of biology and race, it began to take shape as a science, and as a uniquely American science, in the 1870s. Several factors contributed to shifting the study of people and peoples from the realm of natural history to that of anthropology. One was, of course, the reorienting of scientific thinking represented and inspired by the publication of Charles Darwin's *Origin of Species* in 1859 and *The Descent of Man* in 1871. With those works, the idea of evolutionary change, long in the air, crystallized. In 1877, Lewis Henry Morgan, who had been writing studies of Native Americans and others that drew both on Enlightenment environmentalist ideas of progress and on earlier ethnological concerns with biology and race, synthesized his ideas into a theory of cultural evolution in a book called *Ancient Society*.[6]

Morgan's theory was based on the idea, then gaining credence, that societies lent themselves to the same kind of structured analysis that biological organisms did. Morgan understood the science of anthropology, or the study of mankind's beginnings, to be a hard science through which practitioners could deduce natural laws and accurately predict future development. His observation of the Iroquois of his native New York and his study of European history convinced him that all human societies evolved according to set patterns, just as all human beings passed through set stages as they grew from fetus to adult. He posited three hierarchical stages of cultural development: savagery, barbarism, and civilization. Each stage was tied to a progressively more complex method of subsistence that brought with it corresponding social institutions relating to family, government, and property. Hunter-gatherers, with their very small social groups and simple social institutions, one day settled down and became agriculturalists, whose society was more complex. In time, these barbaric farmers developed cities and other accoutrements of civilization, including the most complicated, abstract notions: representative government, nuclear families, private property, and monotheism.

Morgan's theory had three presuppositions. First, human beings were governed by universal patterns of mind. Since all humans had the same basic equipment, it seemed logical to Morgan that, given time, all societies would solve the basic problems of survival in the same way. Shelters would be built, clothing made, food provided—all in ways that were heavily influenced by local environmental factors, until the society evolved enough to overcome the limits of the immediate environment. Second, because they shared universal patterns of mind, all societies were potentially capable of the sophistication exemplified by the Western industrial cultures that stood at the apex of Morgan's scheme, even if at certain historical moments there were major differences in their levels of development. There are traces here both of an Enlightenment faith in the perfectibility of humankind and of the troubling racial thinking that even men as open-minded as Morgan brought to the question of existing social inequalities. Finally, the fact that humans shared patterns of mind and therefore patterns of culture meant that cultures were interchangeable. Contemporary primitive societies were representative of all primitive societies, in all times.

It was the last of these assumptions that helped to give American anthropology its distinctive character. European anthropologists endorsed the idea of an evolutionary scale of cultural development as their American colleagues did. But American anthropologists in search of concrete illustrations for Morgan's narrative found that their own country contained, within its borders, Native American cultures representative of a wonderful range of early phases of development. They thought they had before them the entire history of human social evolution. All they had to do was organize it.

Making the complexities of modern society coherent, giving white Americans of all social classes feelings of control and ownership in a world where both were becoming elusive—these were tasks to which anthropology devoted itself. With its roots in evolutionary theory, fieldwork, and museums, anthropology afforded a three-dimensional sense of order and possession that spoke eloquently to the concerns of intellectuals and reformers. Taking possession of the Native Americans was not an avowed purpose of America's first anthropologists, and yet it was not an accidental outcome of their work, either. They went to the Southwest, as elsewhere, to take an inventory of its inhabitants, and, as surveyors, to map the indigenous cultures in the land. But mapping is a step toward delineation of that which may be possessed, if not to actual possession. As collectors, anthropologists literally dispossessed the Indians of quantities of their material culture, though they did so with the promise to preserve. And as curators they represented native cultures with fixed, captive objects arranged in their own classificatory schemes, placed in buildings that were monuments to the primacy of those who had built them. Showing the nation, in museums and at fairs, what it possessed was an integral part of their work, and their work was important in helping Americans to form a sense of the exceptional nature of their nation.

Despite their often imperialistic patriotism and their hierarchical understanding of human cultural order, the anthropologists, in doing their work, needed not expansive, theoretical statements but closely detailed descriptions. The day-to-day work was not social policy or historical synthesis but cataloging and classifying. So, with the exception of a few grand gestures, anthropologists took possession of the Indians through thousands of small, local acts as surveyors, collectors, and curators. They worked at the research and methodology of their new profession, and had their own personal adventures. But because their profession was enmeshed in the world of popular amusements, they drew the public along with them, and their individual acts resonated far more than those of other, more private scholars.

The ethnologists began by taking inventory, investigating the question of who and what America might be, in the closely detailed genealogical sense used by Frank Cushing in that kiva at Oraibi. At Zuni, Cushing conducted a census, mapped households and families, and made notes on the language. His inventories, combined with the work of other ethnologists, enabled John Wesley Powell and his colleagues in Washington to classify tribes by language stock and to begin to piece together the story of aboriginal migration across the continent. And, as they amassed artifacts to document pre-industrial manufactures, they collected folklore—myths, songs, rituals, customs—that would help to explain them.

Like J. Pierpont Morgan, Louise Havemeyer, and other wealthy patrons who began their art collections in the 1890s, Frank Cushing, Matilda Stevenson, Stewart Culin, and the other salvage ethnologists were caught up in the pursuit of what Neil Harris has insightfully described as "collective possession," playing on the varied, sometimes contradictory meanings of those two words.[7] Culture, a collective property to begin with, was reduced to its collectible parts: rituals, folklore, artifacts, and customs. Turning their own passion for acquisition to the service of science and posterity, they filled museums with the materials from which future generations of anthropologists could derive the history and meaning of the continent's cultures. The great house of the National Museum and other museums became microcosmic representations of the American family. In the process, the anthropologists collected themselves, weaving out of their labors in the field and elsewhere a version of themselves as people who had a place in society and a claim on history. Their individual acts of self-possession, which took the form of, among other things, graceful narratives, painstaking fieldwork, and bold acts of acquisition, in turn influenced anthropology itself, as it claimed its new function in ordering the knowledge of humankind. With a hand in shaping both the professionalism that was an outstanding achievement of this period and the popular nationalist narrative that helped to make Americans comfortable with their baffling urban industrial world, these three found a way to be important.

Matilda Stevenson, Frank Hamilton Cushing, and Stewart Culin viewed their work at Zuni as the preservation of an endangered culture, and in the process of that work they performed neat tricks of transformation. In Zuni's boxlike homes and kivas, they made their measurements, collected their data, and amassed artifacts. Back East, they reconstructed Zuni in box-shaped museum cases, within monumental, ordered buildings. As the photographer and social reformer Jacob Riis fixed the poor starkly but safely within the confines of his photographs, these three ethnologists fixed their Zuni subjects, exposed but unthreatening, behind the glass walls of their exhibition cases. The end result represented not only the Indians but the fact that individual white American adventurers had found their way into the most secret corners of an alien culture and had captured the power of that culture by exploring it.

Stevenson, Cushing, and Culin were inventing their methods as they were inventing an anthropological version of Zuni, and so their stories are simultaneously those of Zuni, of anthropology, of three idiosyncratic Americans, and of America itself. Much of what they collected has been invaluable to the scholars who followed them and, at times, to the Zunis themselves, as they try to stay connected to the world that gave those anthropologists their raw materials. It is now devilishly difficult to separate the anthropologists from the anthropology, and the anthropology from Zuni. What we can do is look at these first tales of Zuni and America, and begin to chart the course by which Zuni came to acquire its shadowy but long-lived hold on the American imagination.

Three

TWO-FOLD ONE-KIND:
MATILDA STEVENSON

—◁∿∿▷—

At the end of 1885, a remarkable houseguest came to stay at the Washington, D.C., home of Matilda and James Stevenson. It was a friend of theirs from Zuni named We'wha. By 1885, Indian delegations were old hat in the nation's capital, but We'wha attracted the enthusiastic attention of Washington society and the press, which delighted in the antics of the so-called Zuni princess. Most other Native American visitors had been men acting in some official capacity to represent their people at the seat of political power in the United States. The "Zuni princess" was a novelty, the first native to move in the world of Washington society women, amusing everyone as she tried to negotiate the customs of that strange culture. For six months, We'wha stayed at the Stevensons' Dupont Circle home, teaching Matilda Stevenson about Zuni religion and folklore, far from the pressures and threats of Zunis who were less comfortable with the idea of an outsider learning their secrets, all the while allowing Stevenson to bask in the limelight, claiming credit for finding this wonderful creature.

We'wha's visit to Washington underscored the porousness of

the boundary between the professional and the popular aspects of anthropology in the early period. Washington, still raw and young in 1885, lacked the old families and old money that typified society in older eastern cities. Its elite included the top ranks of elected officials, bolstered by a somewhat lesser but energetic rank of professionals, among whom scientists were conspicuous, proud of their status and of their high concentration in Washington, which the demands and largesse of the federal government made possible. *Science* magazine, which regularly published items about anthropology, ran a column on "Scientific News in Washington" that confidently placed the nation's capital at the center of the growing faith in science.[1]

Scientific Washington did, indeed, attend to the remarkable Zuni who visited the Stevensons in the winter of 1885–1886. Among the guests at a reception they gave were John Wesley Powell, the head of both the Bureau of American Ethnology and the U.S. Geological Survey; Otis T. Mason, the curator of ethnology at the National Museum; Garrick Mallery, a military man who wrote on ethnological topics; and Albert Gatschet, a linguist of some renown who engaged We'wha to help him with his studies of the Zuni language. We'wha was invited to set up a loom on the Mall and show curious onlookers how to weave blankets, donating the completed ones to the National Museum. In addition, Stevenson took advantage of the stir We'wha created to heighten interest in the Women's Anthropological Society and to loosen the purse strings of those who might be willing to fund ethnological expeditions.[2]

But most of the coverage of We'wha's visit focused on sheer curiosity. The press was enthralled with the exploits of the Zuni, who explored the town on foot and learned to use the railroad tracks to find her way back to the Stevensons' house. We'wha was the star attraction at well-attended receptions, and she mastered the complicated art of calling and receiving; she even bought a red silk parasol, the better to fit into Washington society. Yet she also retained more practical habits from Zuni; one amused reporter told of the wonderful sight of the "Zuni princess" perched on the ridge pole of the Stevensons' house, shoveling snow off the roof. Speaker of the House John Carlisle received We'wha and Mrs. Stevenson, presenting the former with a sack of seeds as a gift, and the two were also the guests of President Grover Cleveland and his sister Rose.[3]

What Washington society and the press, and possibly the Stevensons, did not know at the time was that the "Zuni princess" was a man. We'wha was a berdache. Zuni had a tradition, rooted deep in its mythology, of a third gender that could mediate between male and female, one they referred to as "two-fold one-kind." The spiritual archetype for the berdache seems to be in the long story of the Zunis' journey in search of the Middle Place. Will Roscoe, who has written extensively about We'wha, traces the concept to a part of the tale in which two children of a rain priest, a brother and sister who have been leading the trek, engage in an incestuous relationship. Out of this union the girl gives birth to ten supernatural beings, a man-woman and nine Koyemshi clowns. Angry at her brother, who violated her without her knowledge, she takes the man-woman with her to the kachina village where the dead and the gods live, leaving the clowns behind with their father, her brother. In this story, according to Roscoe, the girl becomes Komokatsik, Old Dance Woman, and the man-woman is her emissary.[4]

On a practical level, a berdache was a man who, upon reaching puberty, decided to identify himself with the women of the pueblo instead of the men. It was partly a matter of personal preference, the berdache choosing to dress and work like a woman because that suited him better than acting as a man. But the decision could also have ritual significance. Like their mythical antecedent, berdaches were expected to be emissaries between Zuni and the kachina village in certain religious ceremonies. So the berdache had to master both the culture of women, with its practices, traditions, and spiritual duties, and the culture of the kachinas, which was generally the realm of men. Like her friend Matilda Stevenson, We'wha was trained to observe and remember, and to negotiate between subcultures that were usually kept distinct.*

Perhaps it is not surprising that, of the three early anthropologists in the pueblo, Matilda Stevenson should produce the most conventional and most conventionally masculine portrait of Zuni. It was she who most openly and perhaps uncritically accepted both the hierarchical implications of anthropology's evolutionary narrative and the link with the federal government that seemed to underwrite an official anthropology. She was a more typical anthropologist than her colleagues, whose intelligence was, in some ways, both more creative and more romantic than hers. Where Frank Cushing wove stories and Stewart Culin evoked the Zuni sensibility in his exhibits, Stevenson collected fragments of its culture and seemed confident that whatever synthesis was necessary would emerge, by itself, from her collection. Her forte was not the narrative but the encyclopedia; her major work on Zuni, a tome of more than six hundred pages, is meant as scientific description, not analysis, though it is marked throughout with her prejudices.

But even descriptions are a kind of story. The Zuni world that Stevenson imagined in those often dry pages was probably shaped as much by a corollary to the evolutionary narrative as by the narrative itself. Lewis Henry Morgan's Enlightenment vision of societies steadily moving up the ladder to civilization and

---

*The English language has no pronoun that describes We'wha. The Zunis used the feminine pronoun; the scholar Will Roscoe resolutely uses the masculine one, in part because of his desire to challenge existing definitions of manhood. I have decided to follow Zuni usage.

equality was premised on the possibility of evolutionary time, but it was apparent even as he wrote that the Native Americans would not be granted such a time. America's first anthropologists believed that social development had been arrested among Native Americans: the evolution of societies could happen only in relative isolation, they thought. In close proximity to a much more highly developed culture like that of the United States, another evolutionary law came into play—survival of the fittest. A basic premise of the salvage ethnology practiced by Matilda Stevenson was the belief that the Zunis, along with other societies, would not survive much longer as a separate culture. Her work, as she saw it, was to make a record of Zuni culture that would outlive the society.

Stevenson imagined a barbaric people. In a scientific sense, this meant that Zuni was a beautiful example of the middle stage of evolutionary development in Morgan's scheme. Settled, agrarian, and capable of a social organization represented by the neatly stacked apartments of the pueblo, the Zunis were congenial evolutionary precursors to the mythical independent farmers who have evoked nostalgia in the United States since the time of Thomas Jefferson. They were more civilized than the savage nomads of desert and plain (though it is worth noting that some of the Plains tribes had given up agriculture in response to an expanding market in buffalo hides tied to eastern industries), and so they nicely represented the possibility of movement on the evolutionary ladder. But the other, more pejorative meaning of "barbaric" also appealed to Stevenson. She saw at Zuni a culture that was superstitious and sometimes cruel, dirty and ill-mannered, and stubbornly resistant to progress. This aspect of barbarism was repellent to her, but also seductive in its exoticism and its hint of danger. It was an important part of the story she told, of herself and of Zuni, that she was a civilized woman among barbarians.

This trope of savagery and civilization was highlighted by the prediction of imminent extinction that hung like a cloud above the unsuspecting heads of these innocent primitives. Although Stevenson decried the Zunis' imperfect adaptation of manufactured goods and other products of American culture, such as alcohol, because they tainted the Zuni culture, often without measurably improving life, there was an air of resignation in her treatise. Her portrait of Zuni had degeneration and loss as one of its motifs. Even the Zunis whom she admired, like the bow priest Nayuchi, she pictured as quaint and increasingly impotent to practice their magic and lead their people. That she herself challenged both their magic and their leadership, and so was agent as well as recorder of the sapping of their authority, she did not question. Stevenson thought she knew how Zuni's story had to end, so she read the lessons of that end into her narrative.

As much as Matilda Stevenson deplored the dirt, the superstition, the lack of manners and refinement, the inability of the Zunis to comprehend the superiority of civilized ideas and practices, she kept going back and inserting herself into the life of Zuni, often aggressively. Something about that life fed a hunger in her. It afforded her a larger measure of autonomy and social importance, gave her a structured walk on the wild side, a chance to be a professional in the service of her government. Only against the red stone of the native Southwest could she make people see her own colors as she did.

Born Matilda Coxe Evans in Texas in 1849, Stevenson had grown up in Washington, in a solidly middle-class family. She and her siblings were taught by her mother, Mary Coxe Evans, and by governesses, and when she was fourteen she went to a "sheltered female seminary" in Philadelphia. But their household must have had, in addition to the domestic shelter that her mother provided, some of the intellectual comings and goings that she sought later in life. Her father, Alexander H. Evans, was

an attorney and a journalist, traveling in the loose world of intellectuals who gathered in the nation's yet unfinished capital. After
five years of formal education, such as it was, in Philadelphia, she
took up not only the study of law with her father but also, informally, the study of chemistry and geology with a professor at the
Army Medical School. She was almost twenty-three when she
married James Stevenson, who was an executive officer for one
of the surveys of the western territories then under way.[5]

In 1879, once John Wesley Powell had convinced Congress to
combine those surveys into the U.S. Geological Survey and provide for an ethnological survey under its auspices, James Stevenson headed west as the officer in charge of the first Bureau of
American Ethnology field expedition. And so Matilda Stevenson, accompanying her husband, arrived at Zuni in a traveling
party that included Frank Cushing and the photographer John
Hillers. James Stevenson's contributions seem to have been primarily administrative, judging from brief descriptions in the writings of his wife and Cushing. Through the army at Fort Wingate,
near Gallup, New Mexico, he arranged for mules to transport the
party from the end of the rail line to Zuni, and later he secured
the use of wagons (made scarce at the fort because of troop
movements) to take their artifacts back to the rail depot. He negotiated for them to use rooms in the governor's house at Zuni,
and he was responsible for meting out the expedition's provisions. His ethnological work consisted of acquiring and cataloging the Stevensons' collection of pottery and making notes on
Zuni social practices, though where his work ended and Matilda
Stevenson's took up is impossible to say.[6]

When Frank Cushing wrote an account of this first visit to
Zuni, he made himself the hero of a story with only one white
person, himself, a stranger in a strange land. In fact, throughout
his five-year stay there was a steady flow of white visitors as well
as residents, missionaries, and traders inside the pueblo or just

outside its walls. At odds with the Stevensons almost from the start of the trip, he relegated these other non-Zunis to the periphery of his adventure story, in which the party arrives after he has made his initial survey of the pueblo, spends a few short weeks gathering artifacts, and then departs early one morning, leaving a trail of dust but none of the provisions it had promised him for his extended stay.[7] Actually, according to Matilda Stevenson, the expedition spent six months at Zuni on that first trip, though it may have been used more as a base camp for visits to other tribes in the region than as a residence. Still, in addition to gathering "treasures, ancient and modern, of Indian art and industry," as Cushing wrote, they were invited to meetings of several secret organizations and observed parts of the autumn Sha'lako ceremony. Despite Cushing's reservations, the Stevensons came to think of themselves as being on friendly terms with the pueblo's inhabitants. They also, between them, made observations that allowed Matilda Stevenson to write a brief monograph on Zuni that was published in 1881, beating Cushing to press—to his considerable annoyance.[8]

Stevenson's account of that first expedition to Zuni differs markedly from Cushing's. For one thing, Stevenson was far more comfortable as part of a government team than Cushing was. Where Cushing painted himself as a solitary adventurer pursuing his mission despite the ineptitude of others, Stevenson began her *Zuñi and the Zuñians* with glowing praise for the personnel of the Atchison, Topeka and Sante Fe Railway, and with special thanks to General William T. Sherman, who apparently took a personal interest in the expedition and arranged for assistance from his officers in the West; to General Edward Hatch, the commander for the District of New Mexico; and to John Wesley Powell for allowing her to draw on Bureau of American Ethnology publications for illustrations for her piece. Where Cushing wrote in the first person, Stevenson for the most part wrote in the more formal and distanced third person, posing as steward for her readers in their introduction to the Southwest, rather than as the subject of an adventure.[9]

Stevenson wrote carefully. The tone was confident, if not comprehensive, and she gave the impression not of taking possession of her new knowledge but of having it to begin with, of already knowing much of what needed to be known about the region. Without benefit of the close textual analysis of Zuni stories that allowed Cushing to write about Zuni prehistory, she nonetheless suggested the broad outlines of the desert's human history. Further research would, she claimed, fill in the details, completing the recovery of "the lost history of the race of men whose record is written in fragments on the cañon walls of Arizona and New Mexico, and whose traditions still speak to us, however imperfectly, through the people now living in the pueblos of that interesting region.[10]

Stevenson was already prepared to give the general outline of that history. The land was, she wrote, "once densely populated, then desolated, and afterward held in precarious tenure by the remnants of a departed race." She suggested that the ancient dwellers in the river valleys of the Southwest "dwelt in peace and prosperity" until they were forced from their homes by some "powerful foe" and fled to the cliffs and caves of nearby canyons to wait out "the cloud of war." They then moved to the more convenient but still easily defensible mesas, and then, still later, back into the valleys once inhabited by their forebears. The present system of pueblos, Stevenson explained, represented the end of the long struggle by the descendants of those ancient people to "regain their inheritance."[11]

Stevenson's prose here was not extraordinary. She was recapitulating a view of the history of the Southwest that other ethnologists, including Lewis Henry Morgan, had already adopted. But in choosing this particular way to set the stage for her trip to

Zuni and what she and her husband found there, she established a tone of quiet antiquity for the region as she asserted her own command of the basic facts. The rest of her thirty-page tract is an odd mixture of observations on Zuni life and custom, sometimes incomplete or erroneous, that were probably drawn from her own experiences and from information culled from white acquaintances. It included an extensive description of ancient and modern pottery styles, for which she probably drew heavily on the notes that she and her husband made for the catalog of items they collected for the National Museum.[12]

Stevenson's first account of Zuni was quiet, matter-of-fact, and largely descriptive. No individual, not even the author, emerges as a real character or subject, though she gives special attention to certain practices that might have been considered odd by her readers—women doing the work of refacing the walls of the pueblo, a relatively large number of albinos, the tradition of taking scalps. Still, this uneven piece of writing established Stevenson's preliminary credentials as an ethnologist. She could now place herself within the yet vaguely articulated world of professional anthropologists.[13]

The brief litany of officials to whom she acknowledged debts—including her husband, an army colonel, an accomplished self-taught geologist, and the leader of the Zuni expedition—gave a highly placed professional sanction to her undertaking. So her claim to being a "voluntary coadjutor in ethnology" had, in part, to do with her association with men of authority, as well as with her own firsthand experience. She used the first-person "I" sparingly but to great effect: "During the summer of 1879 I accompanied the expedition sent out by Prof. J. W. Powell, U. S. Ethnologist, to visit the Pueblos of New Mexico and Arizona for the purpose of studying the habits, customs, etc., of those strange people, and to make such collections of stone implements and pottery as we might be able to obtain." In one sentence, she had connected herself to the Bureau of American Ethnology, to Powell, and to the central purpose of the expedition. She was not just Colonel Stevenson's wife but his assistant.[14]

Stevenson authenticated the ethnological facts not only by her claims as an eyewitness but in reference to objects by picture, accession number, and description. There was very little analysis or conjecture here. It was, rather, a detailed, forthright report of what she saw and what she was told. Had she written only this monograph about Zuni, her claims of being an ethnologist would have been weak, for there was little scientific method in her observations. What gave her work scientific weight was the accompanying catalog of pottery pieces. Having collected and organized these concrete bits of objective evidence, Stevenson could claim possession of a corner of scientific experience.

Stevenson, like other ethnologists in this period before mechanisms for professional certification existed, created her own credentials. She continued to travel to the Southwest with her husband until his death in 1888, adding to her researches on Zuni and on other pueblos in the region. In 1887, Powell included her twenty-two-page report on the "Religious Life of the Zuñi Child" in the bureau's annual report. After James Stevenson died, she drew on the goodwill he had accrued at the Bureau of American Ethnology, as well as on her own knowledge of a study of Sia pueblo they had been working on together, to gain from Powell a temporary appointment to the bureau, an appointment that became permanent in 1890. In the years until her own death in 1915, she regularly made extended visits to the Southwest and wrote a number of works, including four on Zuni, before completing her voluminous study of the pueblo, *The Zuñi Indians*, published in 1904.[15]

Stevenson did all that a woman could do to make herself a

full-fledged member of the Washington scientific community. In addition to her writing, she contributed to Smithsonian exhibits at several world's fairs. She read papers at professional meetings, including the International Congress of Anthropology at the Chicago Columbian Exposition in 1893. She founded and acted as the first president of the Women's Anthropological Society of America, and later, when it opened its roster to women, she joined the prestigious Anthropological Society of Washington. Despite the quality and seriousness of her work, her colleagues at the Bureau of American Ethnology seem to have remembered her primarily as an interloper; and though she could be exceedingly difficult, particularly as she got older, it is unlikely that she was any more imperious or difficult than many other anthropologists. But she was a woman.[16]

What difference did being a woman make in the story Matilda Stevenson created at Zuni? It certainly shaped her sense of herself as a professional, though sometimes in unexpected ways. Like many women, she found more freedom in a new field than in more established pursuits, though she spent time fighting for respect, prestige, and access to meetings and resources. Like her male colleagues, she endured hard, often physically taxing work and rough living conditions as part of the price she paid for her profession. But being a woman could also be an advantage. The best informants about the social connections and daily rituals of life in the pueblo were often women, and in many ways she had better access to them and was more attuned to their work than her male colleagues were. Not that she identified with them! She had internalized a hierarchy in which her position as a white Easterner and a government scientist placed her well above not only the women at Zuni but the men, too. Yet she could travel among the women in a way her male colleagues could not.

It is interesting to speculate on what allure the arduous work of anthropology held for a woman who also craved the attention of Washington society. When Stevenson and her husband returned to the city with We'wha in 1885, they were received by the President and dined with congressmen and other highly placed Washingtonians. She had lived in Washington for most of her life and moved among these men and women, not easily, perhaps, but with a sense of entitlement. She could certainly have stayed home if she had wished to do so.[17] Instead, she chose to accompany her husband and later to travel alone into a part of the country that was often uncomfortable and unwelcoming. She faced the same risks, real and imagined, that male anthropologists faced: dangers from native people who did not understand or approve of what she did and whom she did not understand or approve of; long and difficult exploratory expeditions in which water was uncertain, the terrain difficult, and the directions hazy; strange food; disease; injury; and distance from the world with which she was familiar and on which she depended for supplies and support. She spent months camping out or living in spare quarters, and she often stayed up for days at a time to observe ceremonial dances or to attend important events, such as the birth of a baby or the death of a friend.[18]

Whatever it was that lured Matilda Stevenson to Zuni—adventure, devotion to her work, the promise of prestige, a certain freedom from convention—was not unique to her as a woman. The men who worked at Zuni and elsewhere faced the same challenges and presumably pursued their work for similar reasons. But it may well be that Stevenson found a measure of freedom in the space between her own culture and the ones she studied. At Zuni she was important as an American who had government connections. She could also be a person who played none of the roles circumscribed by Zuni society while she flouted many of the conventions of her own. As a scientist who had the implicit protection of the government, she was relatively free to do as she wished at Zuni. As a white woman with a healthy sense of self-importance, she could order the Zunis around with more success than she probably had with her colleagues at the Bureau of American Ethnology.[19]

It is significant that, from the first, John Wesley Powell and other early anthropologists could easily conceive of a vital role for women ethnologists. The desire to document every aspect of native cultures left men at a disadvantage: though they were more welcome than women in the male world of ritual and ceremony, which offered much dramatic information, the day-to-day customs and gossip of the domestic world, the world of women, was hard for men to penetrate. Powell found the Stevenson husband-and-wife team useful, as did the British anthropologist E. B. Tylor, who visited the couple at Zuni in 1884. In a talk to the Anthropological Society of Washington in which he addressed the peculiarities of American ethnology, of which he generally approved, Tylor noted their contributions, comparing the centralized thoroughness of the government ethnology agency to that of the European Jesuits who had ventured to uncharted regions in an earlier epoch:

> . . . it was interesting at Zuñi to follow the way in which Col. and Mrs. Stevenson were working the pueblo, trading for specimens, and bringing together all that was most valuable and interesting in tracing the history of that remarkable people. Both managed to identify themselves with the Indian life. And one thing I particularly noticed was this, that to get at the confidence of a tribe, the man of the house, though he can do a great deal, cannot do all. If his wife sympathizes with his work, and is able to do it, really half of the work of investigation seems to me to fall to her, so much is to be learned through the women of the tribe, which the men will not readily disclose. The experience seemed to me a lesson to anthropologists not to sound the "bull-roarer," and warn the ladies off from their proceedings, but rather to avail themselves thankfully of their help.[20]

This did not mean, however, that Matilda Stevenson limited herself to the domestic sphere. From the first, she was determined to see all there was to see in the Southwest. With her husband in 1879, she visited some Zuni kivas and was housed with pueblo leaders during the Sha'lako ceremony, though that may have been at least partly so that the Zunis could keep an eye on them both. Much of her reputation for being an intrepid—or pushy, depending on the viewpoint—investigator rested on her apparently fearless attempts to observe and photograph or sketch sacred places and rituals. In 1886, she made the pages of the *Illustrated Police News* beneath the headline

COWED BY A WOMAN

A Craven Red Devil Weakens in the Face of a Resolute Heroine
—Exciting Adventure in an Indian Village in Arizona

The story that followed was accompanied by a sketch of her. Surrounded by her husband and a number of Hopi men, she brandishes her furled umbrella at a dismayed Indian whom she has backed against a wall. The story recounted the Stevensons' attempt to explore a kiva at Oraibi pueblo, the same pueblo that Frank Cushing had invaded two years earlier. The Stevensons had been warned not to enter the kiva, but they did so anyway, and were apparently held captive inside until Thomas Keams, a trader and collector of Indian artifacts, arrived to rescue them. Whatever the facts of the case, which were probably less dramatic and heroic than the *Illustrated Police News* intimated, the story added to Stevenson's reputation for determination and imperiousness.[21]

In any number of other instances, Stevenson bullied her way into ceremonial chambers where she was not welcome; by her own account, she rode roughshod over Zuni guides to make them take her to shrines they wished to keep secret from her.

She reported, without regret or apology, many occasions when Zunis who had supplied her with sacred artifacts or with privileged information expressed their fears of severe punishment, even death, should their contributions become known among other members of the tribe. In one way or another, Stevenson found her way into a remarkable number of secret ceremonies or located informants who were willing to describe them for her.[22]

Gaining the sort of access that she needed in order to assemble the encyclopedic report she produced on Zuni required a good deal more than bravado, however. The bulk of Stevenson's work depended on much more subtle and painstaking methods, and it was here that being a woman may have affected her approach to her science. She worked tirelessly at Zuni, seeking out shrines and other ceremonially significant places, interviewing informants, collecting artifacts, making detailed sketches, and taking photographs. Threats and chutzpah could take her only so far; she had to gain the confidence of at least some of her subjects, and to do that she had to prove her seriousness, through perseverance and hard work, and to make herself a part of Zuni social life. So in addition to working like a man, as one Zuni described it when he invited her to plant prayer sticks with the men one year, she also worked like a woman, taking part in the daily lives and rituals of the owners of Zuni's households. Like her friend the berdache, she lived in both realms.

Much of *The Zuñi Indians* is devoted to Zuni ceremonials and mythology, and Stevenson clearly considered her work primarily to be an investigation of the spiritual aspects of Zuni culture; she subtitled it "Their Mythology, Esoteric Fraternities and Ceremonies." It is almost impossible to separate what she gleaned from personal observation from what she learned from informants. There are no footnotes, and most of her informants are unnamed, possibly to protect them from retribution from other Zunis who felt they had revealed too much. But scattered here and there in the text are clues to how she did the work and the risks that she was willing to take.

One thing she was willing to do was venture out of Zuni in search of shrines and mythologically important places in the countryside. She described several trips that she made with her husband and Zuni guides, including one in which she explored a cave the Zunis believed to be the entrance to Ko'thluwala'wa, the place where the ancestors and gods retire between dance rituals. On her own, she persuaded her guides to take her to see Hanlipinkia, a site inhabited by the gods when they traveled from their place of origin, in the underground fourth world, to the world above and their final destination, the Middle Place.

Stevenson claimed to have been the first American to see that sacred spot, and her journey there was an adventure as exciting as any in the repertoires of her swashbuckling colleagues. She and her guides set out from Zuni twice. The first time, they followed a route that provided no water, and the party had to turn back after several days. On the second try water was more certain, but the terrain was not. Reaching a precarious downhill descent, one of her guides, fearing Stevenson would be killed if she continued to drive her own rig, grabbed the reins and piloted the carriage down the hill without giving her time to think about it. For whatever reason, Stevenson had firmly forbidden the Zunis to touch her wagon, but in this instance she was evidently willing to forgive the transgression. Clearly, she insisted on her independence and was sure of her own abilities as a horsewoman and an explorer, having more confidence in herself, generally, than she did in her native guides.[23]

Matilda Stevenson, like her male colleagues, had a good measure of the adventurer's spirit and arrogance. But she spent a great deal of time, as they did, in mundane activities. Between the lines of her treatise on Zuni there is evidence of a patience as notable as her imperiousness. She spent hours listening carefully to informants as they recited different versions of the society's myths and ceremonial songs, sorting through the variations that always occur in an oral culture. She was equally tireless in observing dance ceremonies and other rituals, many of which lasted for days and nights at a time and some of which required that she sit in an enclosed and smoky kiva. She illustrated her reports with her own ceremonial-dance schemes and with photographs of the many altars used by Zuni's esoteric fraternities, and, in the last years of her work at Zuni, she wrestled unhappily with her typewriter to send regular field reports to her superiors at the Bureau of American Ethnology.[24]

All these activities were becoming routine for anthropologists working in the field. Yet Stevenson's work differed from that of her male colleagues, as her writings on Zuni's more mundane social customs show. As Powell and Tylor predicted, the world of women, keepers of much of the social lore of the culture, was more accessible to other women than it was to men. Stevenson attended to life's most critical passages, birth and death, and to everyday events with the same thoroughness that marked her other undertakings.

Though Stevenson had no children of her own, she was confident enough of her understanding of both pregnancy and childbirth to offer remedies for some of their side effects and to attend even difficult labors, apparently calmly and probably as a participant as well as an observer. In one case, she treated a woman suffering from "a cough and a pain in the right side of her abdomen" with what she described as "simple remedies." In another, she intervened, at the request of an expectant father, to calm the fears of his wife, who had been told by a prominent healer, Nayuchi, that she was carrying a serpent rather than a child, the result of having drunk from a sacred spring belonging to the plumed serpent Ko'loowisi. In this case, as in others, Stevenson succeeded in asserting the lore of her own culture over that of the Zunis. Her actions, rational according to her lights, show her representing an alternative authority in Zuni that may well have pushed a wedge between the Zuni people and their traditional authorities. Her description of these actions reinforced her interpretation of Zuni as a place of primitive innocence and superstition; much as she liked the people and respected leaders like Nayuchi, she felt compelled to speak up when she thought they were wrong.[25]

Stevenson's description of Zuni's birthing customs suggested at least a cursory knowledge of medical terminology and of conditions one might expect Zuni midwives and doctors to encounter. She reported, as if in answer to a list of questions, on swelling of the hands and feet, lacerations of the perineum, blindness caused by childbirth (there was none), sore nipples, constipation, and hemorrhaging. In addition, she dutifully registered mothers' pulse rates, in both routine and difficult deliveries. If she herself took these readings, which seems likely, then she was not merely a silent observer in the corner of the birthing room. Once again, she was telling the story of a culture in need of benevolent intercession.[26]

Where Stevenson gained her nursing experience is not clear. She made a lifelong friend of William Henry Holmes, who later became the head of the Bureau of American Ethnology, when she nursed him through a severe illness, and she seems to have been a competent childbirth attendant. Perhaps her familiarity with this quintessential aspect of the world of women was part of a woman's general knowledge—which suggests deeper dimensions for the Victorian middle-class convention of a "genteel" separate sphere for the second sex. After all, much of women's work was grueling, very physical, and not at all genteel. Certainly, attending childbirth, illness, and death required a stronger stomach, a cooler head, and greater endurance than the sentimental ideal of frail womanhood suggested. Stevenson, who had chosen a life that separated her from what she called civilization for long periods of time, was adept in these less than ladylike but very womanly arts.[27]

In fact, in late-Victorian America, there was a fair amount of fluidity in apparently fixed notions of male and female behavior, and by the first decades of the twentieth century many of those notions had been seriously compromised. In hindsight, Matilda Stevenson's activities at Zuni and in Washington begin to look almost conventional. Like many other women of her time, she worked not only at her job but at making a place for herself and for other women in her profession. In her intrepid forays into the field and in her public work on behalf of anthropology in Washington, she laid herself open to all the usual charges of unfeminine behavior, and it is a tantalizing question whether her friend We'wha did not recognize in her a kindred spirit, a metaphoric man in woman's clothing. Stevenson, like We'wha, occupied a space between the two genders, both in Washington and at Zuni. And that meant that, regardless of her tenacious regard for the conventions of her own culture, she was testing the limits at home as surely as she was at Zuni.

Like many who did what she did, Stevenson was a particular entrepreneurial frontier type, occupying a geographic frontier as well as a scientific and professional one. At Zuni, she roamed the world of men and the world of women, taking on the persona of scientist, invader, adventurer, trader, nurse, friend, and bully, sometimes all at once. In Washington, she was society matron, anthropologist, promoter, interloper—and friend and bully. She was certainly not always ladylike, and she could do great damage with the best of intentions, as when she undermined Nayuchi's authority as a healer or persuaded people to tell her secrets against their better judgment. On the other hand, the Zunis could have thwarted her investigations, but at least one key member of the tribe, We'wha, found her researches useful, and so they were allowed to continue. John Wesley Powell, by all accounts a skillful politician, would have found a way to keep her out of the Bureau of American Ethnology had she been merely a self-important amateur. But Stevenson was neither wholly obtuse about Zuni nor a beacon of enlightened scientific insight, neither a liability for the Bureau of American Ethnology nor the prodigal son that her colleague and competitor Frank Cushing was. She created herself, with Zuni as a background, at a time of flux, pragmatically combining the old-fashioned and modern, personal and professional, feminine and masculine attributes that allowed her to do what she wanted to do.

It is fitting, then, that Stevenson's closest woman friend in Zuni was biologically a man. We'wha became Zuni's most famous berdache, in large part because of her association with Stevenson. But she was also a remarkable individual operating in a remarkable time. She helped Stevenson to acquire the information she wanted about Zuni rituals and to circumvent those in Zuni who tried to exclude her from sacred places. Unlike other informants, however, We'wha seems to have had a social purpose in cooperating with the curious Americans. The early anthropologists were harbingers of change for Zuni, bringing the outside world in with them, speeding the process of cultural miscegenation that endowed their work with such urgency. We'wha studied Stevenson and the United States as carefully as Stevenson studied her and Zuni, apparently looking for a way to negotiate that change that preserved essential parts of the culture by adapting others. She was, Will Roscoe has argued, an "authoritative innovator," a respected person among the Zunis who combined imagination and insight to envision a Zuni that survived its contact with the United States.[28]

It is impossible to know for certain whether We'wha's sense of herself as different, as existing somewhere between male and female in a unique and important third way, influenced her sense of social commitment. Certainly, the Zuni leaders who welcomed Frank Cushing into the Priesthood of the Bow were also searching for ways to mediate the impact of contact with white America. In fact, the Zunis had allied themselves with the U.S. Army against the Navajos before the anthropologists began to study them, so a sense that familiarity might mitigate the threat of the expanding United States seems to have been fundamental to their preservation instinct; this pragmatic approach to encroachments from outside had also marked their dealings with the Spanish. So We'wha, faced with both brutally explicit and more subtle challenges to Zuni sovereignty, may have adopted no more than a traditional stance toward outsiders.[29]

Nevertheless, We'wha is at least metaphorically significant. Her history as a berdache, as a Zuni leader, and as a sort of anthropologist in her own right offers an illuminating counterpoint to the stories of Stevenson and the other anthropologists who made Zuni their quarry. As a boy, he had been raised by an aunt after the death of his parents in an epidemic. When he reached his teens, We'wha elected the role of berdache, choosing to remain in his aunt's female world. Had he chosen the more conventional masculine route, he would have been initiated into one of the Zunis' male kachina societies and, upon marriage, would have left his aunt's household for that of his wife's family. Instead, he joined the women, changing his dress and his pronouns. We'wha now contributed diligently to the work of maintaining the house, preparing food, making pottery, weaving, and attending to the family's ceremonial obligations. In addition, as a berdache, she regularly participated in the Kia'nakwe ceremony, assuming the role of Kor'kokshi, a captured god-warrior who had been forced, according to Zuni tradition, to dress like a woman in order to make him "less angry."[30]

We'wha and Stevenson were about the same age—thirty—when Stevenson first arrived at Zuni in 1879, and over the years their friendship deepened. By Stevenson's account, We'wha was a respected member of the Zuni community. She apparently had quite strict standards and exacted a high level of performance not only from herself but from others in her household. Strong and intelligent, she had a facility with languages that made her useful as a repository of the oral traditions of her culture and a reliable participant in complicated and archaic prayer rituals, and she became invaluable to Stevenson as a source on Zuni practices. Her ear for language and her eye for detail also made her an excellent guest and a shrewd observer of native customs when she went to Washington with the Stevensons in 1885.[31]

Even before the Stevensons came to Zuni, We'wha had associated with Americans from outside the pueblo, doing domestic chores at the Protestant mission school at Zuni, where people believed she was a woman, as Stevenson did perhaps as late as We'wha's visit to the capital. Stevenson borrowed her from the missionaries and tried to engage her to do domestic chores, reporting with rather patronizing humor on her attempts to teach We'wha how to do laundry—a task that We'wha parlayed into a business of sorts, taking in the washing of soldiers and their families who were stationed at Fort Wingate. Significantly, she remained a respected member of Zuni society, where associations with outsiders and especially the accumulation of wealth sometimes occasioned jealousy and even accusations of witchcraft.[32]

We'wha was a gold mine for Stevenson. Not only did she help with the housework but she offered Stevenson detailed access to the domestic female world of Zuni and to information on Zuni rituals that were the province of men. She took Stevenson to local shrines and intervened covertly to help her see and photograph areas of the pueblo that other Zunis blocked. She cast her lot wholeheartedly with Stevenson's anthropological project—whether because of their friendship, a sense of gender kinship, or because she saw Stevenson as a means by which she could preserve threatened Zuni traditions, it is impossible to ascertain.

They must have made a striking pair. Both were dominating personages. We'wha, by Stevenson's accounts, was an impressive person with an authoritative personality. Stevenson, who shared with We'wha a strongly cut chin and a determined, serious mouth, had made herself part of a masculine world and had the force of will to stand her ground there. These two earnest, hardworking, sometimes difficult and demanding friends found in each other something complementary. In their own ways, in their own cultures, they both tried to find stable ground in a shifting world.

We'wha and Matilda Stevenson collaborated on the extensive portrait of Zuni that Stevenson wrote (it was published in 1904, eight years after We'wha's death in 1896), and they had their own reasons for wanting to do so. Each had deeply rooted and sometimes incompatible ideas about what Zuni was and what it was likely to become. They viewed the world from entirely different perspectives, and sometimes their conversations might as well have been in two different languages (as, in fact, they may have been). Still, they found more of use in each other than otherwise.

While most of their time together was spent at Zuni, a good deal about their relationship was revealed during that wonderful visit to Washington that We'wha made in the winter of 1885–1886. For Stevenson, the visit was a professional and a personal coup. Although the press loved the more ridiculous aspects of the Zuni's visit, important people took notice of Stevenson because of We'wha. We'wha was not ridiculous, despite the fun the press had in trying to make her so, and she used her time to study an adversary up close. We'wha did in Washington what Stevenson did at Zuni, boldly exploring everything she could and suspending judgment as long as there were observations to be made. When she went home she did not, any more than

Stevenson did, continue to pursue the practices of the culture she had visited.

This was much to Matilda Stevenson's dismay. She had noted that We'wha's skin actually got lighter in Washington, and seemed to connect that occurrence to the influence of civilization rather than to the fact that the Zuni had left the outdoor life and the bright desert sun for the more sheltered life of the city. We'wha's skin darkened again when she returned to Zuni, and she shed the civilized customs she had adopted in the capital as soon as she returned home. Stevenson associated the one with the other. She had hoped that We'wha's six-month exposure to civilized dining habits would be enough to bring the custom of eating at a table with knives and forks to Zuni. A congressman from Connecticut, she wrote,

> . . . desiring to aid in Christianizing and civilizing the Zuñis, gave to an Indian, who was spending the winter with the writer, a large box of cutlery and silverware, thinking that this Indian, having had the environment of civilization for six months, would carry back its influence to her people. When the writer visited Zuñi about two months after the return of the Indian to her home, she found that the steel knives had been distributed among the rain priests and others, for the purpose of fashioning te'likinawe [prayer sticks], and that the large silver spoons were used with popcorn water, which is drunk in certain ceremonials. The forks were playthings among the children, the Indian to whom the things were given having returned to the use of her fingers in place of the knife and fork. Yet this Zuñian, during her six months' stay in Washington, came in contact only with the highest conditions of culture, dining and receiving with some of the most distinguished women of the national capital.[33]

For Stevenson, this episode demonstrated the futility of attempting to civilize Native Americans. Though the Zunis were capable of imitating the worst aspects of civilization—Stevenson was particularly dismayed by the increase in drinking and drunkenness at Zuni ceremonies—and of making small adaptations in their architecture and dress, Stevenson found little reason to believe that they would ever embrace either Christianity or her standards of cultured behavior. Ultimately, her 1904 study of the pueblo was the record of a culture that she believed would degenerate under the influence of Americans.[34]

Stevenson used We'wha's visit to enhance her connections with important people in Washington, and We'wha explored Washington in search of something that might be of use at Zuni. We'wha may have returned from the city just as disillusioned as Stevenson did from Zuni, though for different reasons. She found little in Washington worth bringing back home except, as in the case of the cutlery and silverware, as interesting variations on objects the Zunis already had. Yet she remembered her stay in Washington fondly, maintaining an affection for those she had met there for the rest of her life. Stevenson reported that photographs and gifts commemorating the Washington visit numbered among the "cherished" possessions that were destroyed ceremonially when We'wha died ten years later. But We'wha also spent her last years at Zuni steadfastly defending local traditions against aggressive incursions from outside. In 1892 she was arrested, along with a number of tribal officials, for interfering with soldiers who had come to Zuni to arrest its civil governor for allowing a witchcraft trial to proceed. The witchcraft trial itself was symptomatic of tensions within the pueblo, related to both the degeneration of traditions and to economic pressures from outside; in the generally consensus-oriented pueblo, misfortunes, individual or communal, were occasionally explained as the result of witchcraft, and in this case the accused witch was a man whose close ties to white Americans and his relative wealth had made him an object of both envy and approbation. We'wha and the others were jailed for a time, and though the religious and

civic leaders of Zuni regained some of their power at Zuni afterward, this episode diminished both their authority and their
prestige. We'wha died a few years later, at the age of forty-seven,
exhausted by the effort to rebuild and decorate her house to re-
ceive the Sha'lako gods during that year's autumn festival. Whatever she learned of white American society in Washington, she
had returned to Zuni committed, even in the face of inevitable
changes, to upholding her culture's most important traditions.[35]

With We'wha's help, Matilda Stevenson wrote a good book
about Zuni, and Stevenson's idiosyncrasies and blind spots do
not negate her contribution to American society and to Zuni,
where people still consult the record she made of practices that
have suffered the passage of time. But if she had a good grasp of
the trees, Stevenson missed the forest. In the end, other things
were more important to her than understanding at a deeper level
what Zuni and her good Zuni friend were really about. She was
content to view Zuni paradigmatically, as the concrete representation of an abstract notion, as the barbaric phase in humanity's
cultural evolution.

The best example of Stevenson's failure to "get it" was the
pièce de résistance of We'wha's tour of Washington, which was
described beautifully by Will Roscoe in his biography of the
berdache. This was an annual fund-raising event called a kermis,
after an old Flemish custom of yearly fairs and carnivals that was
borrowed in turn-of-the-century America by the sponsors of
charity events. In 1886, there was a kermis in Washington that
consisted of an evening of choreographed tableaux organized
around the theme of a "gathering of nations," as befit a country
that was curious about its relationship to the rest of the world.
The entertainment in the National Theater included a range of
exotic performances, including dances on Japanese and Gypsy
themes. Significantly, though, the dance meant to represent
America at this gala was Native American, and Matilda Steven-

son was among the volunteers responsible for that part of the program. It was performed by twenty-five couples of unmarried men and women from Washington society—and Stevenson's guest from Zuni.[36]

The kermis dance represents better than anything else the blend of sincere concern, curiosity, and superficiality that marked the odd symbiotic relationship between Stevenson and We'wha, and between professional and popular anthropology of the time. The dance itself was largely stereotypical. Choreographed by a Professor Marwig from New York, it seems to have aimed at being a generic Indian dance that satisfied the public enthusiasm for "wild Indians." The young white dancers performed in bronze- or blackface, clothed in feathers and wielding tomahawks; press descriptions suggest something closer to Apaches or Plains tribes than people from the pueblos. And yet, at the center of the event, taking it all very seriously, was We'wha.[37]

We'wha believed the dance was a sacred undertaking, akin to those at Zuni, and though she did not fully understand the significance of this one, once she had agreed to participate she danced as solemnly as she would have at Zuni. On the other hand, the young men and women who danced with her probably did so with a mixture of seriousness and fun: it was a society event with exotic costumes and conduct that was just a bit risqué for people of their race and class. Somewhere in the middle were Professor Marwig, who seems to have wanted his dance to be both educational and inspiring, and Matilda Stevenson, who was able simultaneously to exploit the sensation of We'wha's presence and to advance her own career, which she believed was of consequence to her profession and her country.[38]

It would be easy to condemn the kermis Indian dance as frivolous and exploitative. To a large extent, it was. But it was also a sincere, if misguided, attempt to pay tribute to an aspect of America that seemed somehow to represent the nation itself.

The nation was a century old, and these people at the heart of the capital were grappling, in an unsophisticated way, with a perplexing problem: What represented the whole nation? What distinguished this nation from the European nations that had contributed such dances as the minuet, which had been performed earlier in the program? If the program called for an *American* dance, what ought that dance to be? The choreographer of the Indian dance billed it as "the national American dance," and intended the Indian figure in it to be "the first representation of this national figure." It may well be, as Roscoe has suggested, that the message here was not about Indians but about the conquest of savagery by civilization. In any case, whether or not they were aware of the weighty claims it was supposed to make, the performers and the audience recognized the dance as quintessentially American.[39]

The dance served another purpose, too. As fractured as was its representation of Native Americans, the dance struck a responsive chord. Given dignity, authenticity, and an air of exoticism by We'wha's presence, the performance was a terrific piece of public relations, exciting interest in both Native Americans and Stevenson's anthropology. Matilda Stevenson's ethnological work with We'wha during the Washington visit was important, but most of it could have been done as well at or near Zuni. However, as an ongoing spectacle designed to enhance Stevenson's status as a scientist and in society, and to keep Washington's interest engaged in anthropological work among Native Americans, We'wha's visit was especially important. In an age in which spectacle had begun to replace more sober cultural forms, an extended performance, like We'wha's visit, joined more confined spectacles, like mannequin Indians in anthropological displays at world's fairs, in challenging the thoughtful scientific tone of written anthropology and the narrative claims of evolutionary theory. In the short run, such spectacle greatly enhanced anthropology's scope; in the long run, the concessions made to popularity helped to undermine its quality.

We'wha and Matilda Stevenson appear to have been genuine friends. Thoroughly committed to the cultures to which they were born, they were nevertheless curious about others and willing to take significant risks to learn more about them. Their goals were different, yet in the end they were perhaps not so far apart. Putting aside the ethnocentrism of these remarkable characters, their means were complementary even if their ends were not. We'wha wanted to safeguard her society and its traditions against the very real threat posed by both friendly and hostile American outsiders. Though many within Zuni opted for isolation, for excluding observers, and for carefully shielding the secrets of their metaphysical and physical worlds, We'wha traveled another route. She may have been more fatalistic than the others. Fearing that change would come regardless of what her people did, she may have concluded that it made more sense to try to direct the change than to fight it outright.[40]

She found an ally in Matilda Stevenson, for all Stevenson was convinced that she, not We'wha, was in charge. Stevenson's monograph on Zuni was an extraordinary record of a period in Zuni history that had passed by the time she published it, and We'wha's help was essential. Much that might have been lost to the Zunis survives within that voluminous report. That Stevenson and other ethnologists like her were also in large part responsible for Zuni's inability to hang on to important pieces of its history and tradition, and for the Zunis' subsequent dependence on ethnological works for information about their own culture, is one of the more pointed ironies at the heart of the practice of salvage ethnology that Stevenson typified. She was responsible for removing hundreds, perhaps thousands, of artifacts from their social context, and the methods she used—theft, bullying, and taking advantage of the poverty of the pueblo—did as much to undermine the integrity of the Zuni social structure as did the wholesale purchase of its material culture. She sought to save Zuni by dismantling it.

Embedded within Stevenson's textual representation of Zuni, as within the collection she made for the National Museum, was her conviction that some vital truth about Zuni culture in particular and human culture in general would emerge if she assembled enough pieces. She assumed that those pieces would fill in the outline of that paradigmatic barbarian society that the evolutionary narrative had sketched. In fact, despite her pose as an objective recorder of information, her own story wove its way in and out of her long detailed descriptions of religious ceremonies and social customs, and in the end her story of Zuni can be understood only through her lens. Between the covers of her Bureau of American Ethnology report, she packaged not only a record of Zuni society over twenty-odd years but some messages for her own society as well.

A prevailing theme—more structural, perhaps, than textual—was that Zuni, though (to her eyes) uncivilized, could be comprehended by outsiders, could be captured within the covers of a book. (It is interesting to try to imagine a similar book about the United States.) As elusive as culture might be, Stevenson claimed to offer a comprehensive record of this particular culture at a particular point in time, though she acknowledged that there was still much work to be done. The portrait she drew of Zuni, with its complex, integrated system of spiritual beliefs, was of an extremely rational, well-ordered society of societies, doomed because its rationality and order served a worldview that she could not see as other than superstitious. The Zunis she wrote about, many of them with much affection, were for the most part friendly, amusing, and respectful of her and, by extension, of her government. And limited. With barely perceptible sleights of hand, she dismissed and belittled what she reported of Zuni medical lore, for example, or of its spirituality or social customs.

Stevenson's work is a mainstay of Zuni anthropology, yet it

earns little more than a footnote today in the history of anthropology. The profession took a different course, rejecting, especially, her hierarchical view of cultures. By the time of her death in 1915, university-trained anthropologists had taken over the field. In that year Alfred Kroeber, one of the first anthropologists of this generation, visited Zuni to begin his study of kin and clan relationships. Though much remained the same in how anthropologists worked in the field, the time of the self-trained, self-proclaimed professional was over. Stevenson became an example who was studied because she had historical knowledge that could not be recovered except through her written work, but she was reviled as essentially unprofessional because she did her work before the discipline had established its credentials. In her day, however, Stevenson accomplished a great deal. Against imposing odds, she established herself as a professional, trained herself to observe and record, and obtained for herself a berth in what was then the most prestigious institution for anthropologists in the United States. She built this career piece by piece, while collecting the myriad fragments that made up her portrait of Zuni.

Four

A PLACE OF GRACE:
FRANK HAMILTON
CUSHING

—⟪⟫—

At Zuni, in the autumn of 1890, you could have found a man preparing for one of the ceremonial dances that were the dramatic expression of the Zunis' understanding of the relationship between the natural and the supernatural worlds. Like the other members of his fraternity, he would have removed his molded, carved kachina mask from the protected place within his household where it was cared for ritually throughout the year. In a kiva in the pueblo, or at some secret place out across the flat plain that Zuni occupies, this man would, following patterns he had patiently learned, don the mask, paint, shells, and rattles that briefly transformed him into the kachina god he impersonated. For hours or days he lived between two worlds, in a fleeting place of grace where the spiritual took concrete form and he was simultaneously a man and a god.

At about the same time, in an American city nearly a continent away, you might have found another man involved in another transformation. Somewhere in Washington, D.C., perhaps in the offices of the red-brick Smithsonian castle or in the back halls of the National Museum, Frank Hamilton Cushing, who

75

had recently spent nearly five years among the Zunis, shed the sober garments of the urban middle class, peeling off the suit jacket and pants, the shirt, the underclothes; he, too, then dressed himself as a Zuni god. A breechcloth, an anklet, and a painted mask effected the transformation. Then, dressed as a Zuni dressed as a supernatural creature, he posed for a series of photographs.

Officially, what Cushing was doing was putting his scientific knowledge at the service of artists who were making mannequins for an exhibit of some of the artifacts he had collected. A number of anthropologists and curators were experimenting with what they called the "life group," a museum form that, they believed, better evoked the people who had created the artifacts than did rows of glass cases crammed with specimens. Even Franz Boas, who was deeply troubled by the excesses of evolutionary anthropology, posed for photographs that would allow mannequin artists to reproduce authentically the gestures of Native Americans from the Pacific Northwest coast. Yet Cushing's photographs, and others like them in which Cushing assumed other Native American identities, suggest something more than a commitment to authenticity. At the heart of the photographs, and at the heart of the exhibits that were built from them, Frank Cushing put his own body, himself, a self that was more than just an anthropologist who had lived among, studied, and come to respect the Zunis.

In the course of his years at Zuni in the 1880s, Cushing found a variety of ways to blur the line between himself and the Zunis: he practiced their arts, explored their landscape, and, finally, induced them to initiate him into the Priesthood of the Bow, which made him, at least ceremonially and sometimes more practically, a member of Zuni's governing council. When he put on the clothes of a Zuni and a kachina god in Washington, he was doing more than merely posing, more than just playing Indian. In some fundamental way, he felt himself to be a Zuni, as the Zuni man dressed as a mudhead or a Sha'lako god felt himself to be that god. The experience was simultaneously acting and transformation. Cushing, in the process of his anthropology, appropriated something intangibly Zuni, something that was as important to him as being a scientist at the Smithsonian.

The idea of Zuni that Cushing reified in his anthropological stories differed from the paradigmatic dying culture Matilda Stevenson recorded. It existed more or less independently of outside influences, a cohesive world unto itself, a complete cultural system bound, metaphorically at least, by the walls of the pueblo. For Cushing, whose method was that of total immersion, Zuni was the living backdrop for an adventure possible in the 1880s but more difficult to imagine today. Armed with the science and technology of his own culture but lacking the self-reflection that is a standard tool of present-day anthropologists, Cushing lived at Zuni for years, playing with his own identity as he plumbed the depths of Zuni identity. Empathetic, imaginative, craving the life of the Indian as well as the life of the scientist, he experienced Zuni as a sort of magical amusement park full of puppets without strings.

When Cushing wrote about Zuni, both popularly and professionally, he put himself into the story so that his readers, too, could feel the mystery of the transformations he described. Whether it was the tale he told in his more famous work, a magazine series entitled "My Adventures in Zuñi," or in anthropological studies of pottery styles or arrow manufacture, Cushing reported not only on what he had learned but on how he had learned it. And he learned by doing, by living with the Zunis, and by becoming, in careful ways, one with them. The Zuni culture that Cushing imagined for his readers was a sort of stage set of a strange land in which appeared living, sometimes dangerous adversaries whom he mastered and tamed.

The Zuni intangible that Cushing appropriated, as he transformed himself at will into a Zuni and then back into a scientist, was, I believe, that place of grace that Jackson Lears has so perceptively identified as an absence that was at the core of the strange nostalgia that accompanied Americans' confidence in progress and modernity at the turn of the century. Even as they welcomed progress, many Americans experienced a deep spiritual uncertainty, and it is no accident that at the same time that science became the lingua franca of American business, politics, and even amusement, Americans often sought out spiritualists, phrenologists, and other mystical practitioners. They were searching for this place of grace, this fleeting, ungraspable place. Within his science, Cushing could, occasionally, inhabit it. More important, he could, in his writings and in the exhibits that he posed for, re-create the moments when he experienced it. This was not grace itself, of course, but the evocation of it, the memory of it. The popularity of anthropology exhibits, then and now, is partly grounded in a desire to apprehend, as Cushing did, the moment of transformation.

By his own design, Frank Hamilton Cushing was the first ethnologist to enter Zuni, edging out even Matilda Stevenson, who more or less traveled with him. As a member of that first official expedition sponsored by the Bureau of American Ethnology in 1879, he could claim to be among the first anthropologists to live and work professionally among native peoples. Certainly his extended stay in the pueblo, when he acted as both observer of and participant in an unfamiliar culture, marked him as a pioneer in the new discipline. But he was also a maverick, an adventurer, and an innovator, and as such achieved both his contemporary success and popularity and his more recent obscurity. Cushing was a careful observer and an intrepid explorer, and he made invaluable contributions to the study of Native American cultures, but in his powerful attraction to the art of the narrative he sometimes sacrificed scientific objectivity to his desire to create wonderful stories.[1]

In this, though it later helped to discredit some of his work, he was perfectly suited to the spirit of his own age and culture. In a science that dealt in fragments, he had the ability to create wholes that not only worked well as stories but fit well into the guiding evolutionary narrative. In a culture that still thought of history in linear, progressive terms, loved a good adventure, and thrived on the voyeuristic first-person narrative, he wrote adventure stories in which he was the hero and wrote up his ethnological investigations as if they were mystery stories, drawing his readers step-by-step through the progress of his discoveries. He was able to weave, out of the slenderest threads of prehistoric evidence, synthetic wholes in which the patterns seemed sure and strong.

Cushing's gifts made him perfect for anthropology. At the heart of evolutionary anthropology lay the assumption that the human mind was guided by universal, not culturally specific, impulses, and thus that everyone facing a given challenge under given conditions would arrive at essentially the same solution. This assumption had two important methodological implications. First, it allowed ethnologists to reason by analogy, and to do so with the same certainty with which they reasoned deductively from observation. Because they believed that all societies evolved through similar stages, developing similar or at least comparable technologies and social institutions along the way, they were perfectly comfortable studying ancient Native American cultures by proxy, deducing their histories from the present lives of people who occupied the same rung on the evolutionary ladder. The conviction that ancient and contemporary aboriginal peoples might be considered virtually identical allowed the scientists to call their work an empirical science despite the absence of the actual subject matter they claimed to be analyzing.

Second, when the contemporary peoples could not answer their questions, the ethnologists' belief in the basic universality of the human mind allowed them to stand in for their subjects. Given the structural conditions of a culture—the climate, the terrain, and the available tools—they believed they could work out for themselves, by trial and error, the processes that ancient artisans had developed.[2]

Some anthropologists focused primarily on the imperative to preserve, to collect artifacts and record folklore. Cushing, too, was a tireless collector and observer, but what distinguished him from his colleagues was the extent to which he exploited the ideas of analogy and universality at the core of their evolutionary theory. He was absolutely sure that his own intuition, guided by history and experimentation, was sufficient to fill the gaps in the prehistorical record of the people he studied. His forte was his willingness to speculate about the origin of things. He combined research and what was called re-creation, the reproduction of a lost art by a scientist equipped with the materials available to early people and confident that he knew the universal patterns of mind with which they would have approached them. When artifacts and informants could not answer his questions, he "re-created" the circumstances and allowed his own intuition to supply the missing links.

The arrogance of Frank Cushing's method was part of his personality. At best, it was part of his genius; at worst, it brought charges that he was a charlatan. On at least one occasion, as a member of the Hemenway South-West Expedition in the late 1880s, he trod perilously on the line between re-creation and outright fraud, manufacturing or "improving" an ancient jeweled frog that he claimed he had found. This arrogance seems to have been something he cultivated at a very young age. Among Cushing's most revealing stories was the one he apparently told his friends and colleagues during the course of his professional life—

the outlines of an autobiography—which emerged in the memorials delivered by prominent members of the profession upon his death in 1900.[3]

The 305th meeting of the Anthropological Society of Washington, a distinguished group in the city that was still the center of professional anthropological study, was held in 1900 in memory of Cushing, who had been its vice president. Memorials included tributes by all three men who ran the Bureau of American Ethnology in its prime, Powell, Holmes, and W. J. McGee. Out of bits of Cushing's childhood story, bits that must have come from Cushing himself, Holmes and Powell painted a portrait of an innate professional genius, a man possessed of natural empirical training who had gained his credentials without benefit of much structured or standardized study. With the same facility that allowed him to create history out of Zuni myth and custom, Cushing had told his own boyhood story so that it confirmed his destiny as a professional anthropologist.[4]

William Henry Holmes's recollections of what he knew of Cushing's childhood were shaped partly by the conventions that Theodore Roosevelt had made popular, conventions that stressed the virtues of a strenuous life, and partly by a desire to prefigure Cushing's career in his childhood. According to Holmes, Cushing weighed a pound and a half at birth, "a mere mite of humanity," to which extraordinary fact he attributed some part of Cushing's keenly intuitive intelligence; Cushing apparently claimed that he could "remember faces seen and aches felt" during his first year or two, when "he grew but little, and was kept always on a pillow." Because his size and weakness kept him from close association with his "boisterous" brothers and sisters, he sought, instead, to explore the world alone.[5]

Holmes found evidence of Cushing's predisposition to archaeological research, experimentation, and "experiences with an unsympathetic environment" as early as the boy's ninth year.

He evoked memories of Cushing's linguistic work among the Zunis when he suggested that the dictionary the boy found among his father's books was a powerful influence. Not only did Cushing pore over the volume far into the night, seeking complements to his meager schooling, but he carried it with him on walks through the forest, balancing it on his head. This exercise, practiced "frequently and persistently," had the effect of curing his congenital weakness, transforming his body into one as "straight as an arrowshaft and lithe as the young saplings, his brothers." As he did later, at Zuni, Cushing communed easily with nature. He used the dictionary—presumably an English one—as the basis for sermons that he preached, Holmes said, "to his elder brothers, the trees." As at Zuni and other Indian communities, Cushing apparently felt not only that he understood his audience but that they understood him. "The child was so near Nature," Holmes wrote, "that he conversed with her without fear of misunderstanding, a relation not existing with any human creature."[6]

As a child, Cushing was given to solitary walks and odd experiments that raised eyebrows among his neighbors in central New York State, like fashioning wooden wings and trying to fly from a hayloft. His career as a traveler and a scientist seems to have begun when an itinerant lecturer came to town to teach geology. Cushing, who had long been fascinated by Indian relics, now began to seek geologic specimens as well, and he looked for them farther afield. To earn money for his travels, he "pull[ed] beans for the neighbors." With what small cache he could assemble, he struck out, as intrepidly as he later undertook his first trip to Zuni, and equally without plan or foresight. With a budget of ten cents a day, as short of food as he would later be at Zuni, he traveled around Lake Oneida, piloting a rowboat that was far too heavy for a single boy, until a thunderstorm drove him ashore. Wet and hungry, he pounded on the door of a strange farmhouse and was welcomed in once the suspicious family realized it was only a little boy. Elsewhere in his travels he was treated with less kindness, but he had his adventure and returned home with "valuable collections," a foreshadowing of Zuni adventures to come.[7]

In his teens, Cushing began to acquire associations and experiences that allowed him to think of himself as more than a somewhat eccentric amateur. Learned neighbors instructed him in geology and archaeology, including Lewis Henry Morgan, with whom he apparently conversed as he read Morgan's writings. He also "found his way to Ithaca," where, according to Holmes, he impressed the geologist and archaeologist C. F. Hartt with his uncanny ability to find artifacts where no one else could. Hartt took him in as a student for a "special course of study," though Holmes did not elaborate on its contents.[8]

More of the Cushing story—or myth—emerged in other reminiscences delivered at the same meeting. John Wesley Powell remembered that one of those helpful neighbors, L. W. Ledyard, was a friend of Spencer Baird, the secretary of the Smithsonian, and arranged for the seventeen-year-old Cushing to submit a piece of writing to Baird, who was impressed enough to have it published in the Institution's annual report for 1875. This early letter, Powell claimed, showed that Cushing "knew how to observe significant facts and to compel them to tell their story."[9]

Though Cushing continued to pose as a self-sufficient loner throughout his career, he also clung tenaciously to his professional contacts, particularly those, like Spencer Baird, who gave him a sense of professional standing without interfering in his work. For all his aloofness, he craved both professional and popular attention, and he was jealous of his credentials. Since there was, as yet, no agreed-upon standard for anthropological certification, he had to convince people that the combination of his natural inclination and his experience had earned him a secure place among the pioneers in the discipline.[10]

Cushing's work at Zuni established him in that rank. From the beginning, he controlled the narrative of his coming-of-age as an anthropologist with shrewd artistry. His earliest publications were not scholarly but popular, among them the three pieces in *The Century* entitled "My Adventures in Zuñi."[11] Compressing events of several years into a single yearly cycle, Cushing's articles simultaneously brought Zuni cultural practices to the attention of American readers and heralded his daring and imaginative methods of inquiry. A graceful writer working creatively within the tradition of travel journals, Cushing wrote a marvelous adventure story with himself as hero. The plot involved mystery—the uncovering of closely guarded secrets—as well as danger, and the exploits of the daring young anthropologist were punctuated with descriptions of wonderful ceremonies involving magnificent, if somewhat menacing, costumed figures and a panoply of animistic gods.

According to Cushing, he first saw the Zuni pueblo from a distant mesa in Mal Pais, the lava bed of an ancient volcano that later became home to Aldous Huxley's imagined Zunis in *Brave New World*. Having traversed two-thirds of the continent by rail and much of New Mexico by mule, the twenty-two-year-old ethnologist stopped at the edge of a lava cliff and surveyed the broad, flat valley that lay before him. He drank in the desert's vast distances, its majestic colors and rock formations, and tried to see it as an enormous, detailed relief map of an unknown but enticing region. Adjusting his focus to one small part of the expanse, he traced the course of a small winding river, "the track of an earthworm," from the rock wall and sand hills below him "westward through the middle of the sandy plain and out almost to the horizon," where the river disappeared into "the southern shadows of a terraced hill." From his distant vantage, Cushing saw the hill infused by the light of a sunset on a September evening. He marveled at what appeared to him as "a little island of mesas, one upon the other, smaller and smaller, reared from a sea of sand, in mock rivalry of the surrounding grander mesas of Nature's rearing." Only when he detected movement at the top did he begin to suspect that this was indeed an imitation of nature, "a city of the habitations of men."[12]

The city was Zuni, Cushing's immediate destination and the beginning of an extraordinary anthropological adventure. Armed with a vague mandate from Spencer Baird to "find out all you can about some typical tribe of Pueblo Indians," Cushing surveyed the area and made his choice, mentally fixing the boundaries of the pueblo and staking his claim to its secrets.[13] Some early ethnologists focused on collecting artifacts, traveling only as long as it took to acquire and crate the curious items of ancient and recent manufacture they found in Indian villages. The party with which Cushing ventured to Zuni, headed by Colonel Stevenson, was essentially just such a collecting party. But Cushing, whose mandate came not from John Wesley Powell but from Baird, turned his inchoate desire to learn about Pueblo Indians into a five-year experiment in the defining of anthropological fieldwork. Making it up as he went along, Cushing invented for himself a remarkable persona, an ethnological observer who probed the social and ceremonial spaces of Zuni pueblo armed with little more than notebooks and sketching pencils. When the rest of the expedition packed up and moved on after a few weeks, Cushing elected to stay behind, living alone among the Zunis in an effort to learn all that he could about their culture.[14] He moved into a Zuni household, adopted Zuni dress and diet, and slowly insinuated himself into Zuni social life. Cushing was a very early "participant-observer" in a discipline that grew up around this concept.

The process by which he gained access to Zuni, first as observer and then as participant, was a central theme of "My Adventures in Zuñi." Like other anthropologists, he measured his success in terms of the access he gained to private and sacred aspects of the culture he was studying. In this popular, retrospective look at his first years among the Zunis, he reconstructed for his readers his progress from alien outsider to Zuni intimate in essentially spatial terms. The spaces in the pueblo lent themselves particularly well to his literary device. The village itself, visible from a good distance, was compact and self-contained. Cushing was not yet acquainted with the outlying farming enclaves and the distant mythological geography, so he could rein in his mule atop the lava cliff and comprehend the whole of the community's external facade and its architectural outlines. Moving in closer, he began to see the details, noting the remarkable terracing of apartments and the carefully enclosed gardens and corrals around them, all of which gave him a sense of a bounded society—the more so because he had yet to see any human inhabitants of Zuni. As luck (or literary device) would have it, all the Zunis were gathered together on the rooftops to watch ceremonial dancers in the pueblo's central courtyards.[15]

Just outside the pueblo, still alone with the architecture, Cushing scanned the intricate structure again, fastening more closely on the walls and roofs. His careful eye strained for evidence of human life in the pueblo. Chimneys made of earthen pots suggested Oriental spires, but they also indicated human occupancy. So, too, the heavy ladders protruding through holes in each roof. Small doorways and windows that "pierced the walls of this gigantic habitation" completed the picture. Unable yet to penetrate these inner spaces, Cushing recorded his first impressions with intriguing detail. Windows and doors, ladders and chimneys, all offered the promise of interesting life hidden within. The interiors beckoned to Cushing.[16]

At first, Cushing was confined to the spaces that were open to view. He entered the pueblo at last, dismounting his mule, climbing a "refuse-strewn hill," and then, apparently without interference or invitation, scaling the "two or three ladders leading up to the housetops." Cushing's presence on the rooftop eventually drew the attention of the Zunis. To the sound of rattles and drums, he advanced toward them, finding himself "suddenly confronted by forty or fifty men, who came rushing toward me with excited discussion and gesticulation." Having encountered on Mal Pais a Zuni man who, in greeting, had clasped his hand and breathed on it, Cushing repeated the gesture. This was enough, in his telling, to persuade the Zunis to allow him to join the rooftop assembly, and with that he came, finally, "face to face with nearly the whole population of Zuni." As he had earlier surveyed the whole of the city from atop the mesa, he now took in at one glance the whole of the people who inhabited it. His work during the following years would consist of pursuing the latter through the former, positioning himself first in Zuni's public spaces, then finding his way through its private family spaces to the sacred kivas, the most mysterious of the areas enclosed by the adobe walls, the ultimate prize in Cushing's quest.[17]

In the days that followed, Cushing roamed through the pueblo, but he was frustrated in his efforts to get closer to the center of things. Dogs blocked his access to some of the alleyways he hoped to go down, and the curious heads that popped out at the sound of his shoes on their roofs as quickly disappeared. He had to content himself with further broad views. From the top of the pueblo he surveyed the surrounding countryside, again mentally mapping the terrain. He pictured Zuni as the hub of a wheel, its spokes radiating toward the outlying mesas and hills. He had earlier perceived a village isolated within a grand uninhabited desert, but now he noticed signs that the Zunis had long since imposed themselves on the land. The worn paths that reminded him of the spokes of a wheel indicated long use, and further investigation revealed that Zuni farmers moved constantly to and from their farms with the produce they coaxed from their desert fields. Cushing was beginning to get a sense that the Zunis in fact possessed the landscape, that it was full of socially produced spaces.[18]

But the main story, and the real mission, lay within the walls of the pueblo. The early parts of his *Century* articles convey his urgent and powerful need to find a way into both the private and the sacred spaces of the city, and they chronicle the ethnologist's movement from the pueblo's outer walls to its inner sanctums. He first settled a quarter of a mile away from the pueblo, on the grounds of a mission school, in a tent that he shared with the party's photographer, John Hillers, who made his own photographic record of the pueblo as his contribution to the expedition. Ever the Victorians, the two men symbolically took possession of this small part of the landscape by furnishing their tent. Cushing "spread blankets over the ground, hung pictures and toilet-case on the wind-swayed walls, and thus, with a trunk in either corner, a cot along either side . . . made a snug little home. . . ." But his claim to his cozy home was tenuous. Shortly after the two men had settled in, the privacy of their tent was invaded by a group of Zuni men, who, foreshadowing Cushing's later invasions of their homes and kivas, invited themselves in to sit and smoke and observe their visitors.[19]

Cushing early realized that he could not learn what he wanted to know about Zuni society as a visitor from outside. He sought to gain the confidence of the Zunis by befriending their children, giving them gifts of sugar and trinkets, and taking "the less shy and dirty of them" affectionately in his arms. Though these gestures earned him a pleasant tolerance, they still left him excluded from the ceremonies that were his primary objective. And so he made the decision, possibly within the first week, to "try living with the Indians." He moved "books, papers, and blankets" into the house of the civil leader of the pueblo, Governor Palowahtiwa. There he made himself another snug home, laying his blankets on the floor and slinging his hammock from the rafters, announcing his possession of the space once again by furnishing it.[20]

Now Cushing could extend his observations of Zuni culture from the public exterior of the pueblo to the private interior. He characterized the move as impetuous and aggressive, casting himself as a hero who was willing to defy common courtesy and potentially hostile hosts in the pursuit of his science. The acquisition of a scientific vantage point, which might have occurred less obtrusively, became, therefore, an act of invasion, a conquest of Zuni space, an act of possession that had ramifications outside the pueblo. In fact, however, a closer reading of Cushing's texts reveals a less dramatic story: the room into which he moved his things, apparently uninvited, had already been "secured" by James Stevenson for the use of members of the expedition as they made their collections. A more accurate description might well be that Cushing moved himself into a rented room.[21]

If the move was not quite as heroic as Cushing portrayed it, it nevertheless set him apart from his colleagues, who disapproved of his move into the pueblo, and who subsequently left him behind when they went on to explore other parts of the region. They left him without the provisions he had expected, so the greatest danger he faced was not hostility from the Zunis but the possibility that they would not take pity on him. By his own account, the governor and his family were not enthusiastic about his arrival in their midst, but in the end they took him in, as had the upstate New York family who had found him, as a boy on his first exploring trip, wet and hungry at their door.[22]

Cushing's move into the governor's house gave him his first extended chance to study a Zuni house and Zuni family life. His article first gave an architectural description of the large room he had appropriated—its dimensions, its whitewashed walls and well-swept floor, its huge rafters and roof entrance, its windows and interior doors, its adobe bench and stone fireplace. He then noted the objects that marked this space as domestic: corn-grinding mills, blankets and clothing, hunting equipment, earthen cooking pots, stools, bedding robes, and rugs.[23]

Cushing tells the story of what happened to him during the course of the following year in this domestic space with a certain amount of humor, inviting his readers to glimpse intimate moments of Zuni family life while sharing his own adventures in dodging the attempts his Zuni hosts made to incorporate him into the family and the culture. He wanted very much to be an insider, but he meant to submit to Zuni customs on his own terms. He jealously and furtively protected his own sense of propriety, drawing the line, for example, at courting a Zuni woman, and insisting with equal care on his prerogative, as a scientist, to participate in and observe whatever he wished. The complicated negotiations he undertook through this potentially hazardous cultural maze were gentle domestic adventures compared with the aggressive encounters he had outside. At the same time, his whimsical tale provided a detailed survey of Zuni types and customs, a map of the subtle rules governing family and social life.[24]

Cushing lived in the governor's household as an odd, omnipresent shadow, steadfastly occupying his hammock while the family continued to use the room. The governor held nightly meetings by the fire, and Cushing, in his hammock, eavesdropped, honing his still clumsy ear for the language. From his hammock, too, he observed the courting of a young girl in the family, reporting on the kisses and rebuffs that punctuated the intimate drama on the hearth.[25]

By the beginning of the second of the *Century* articles, Cushing was writing as an insider, shifting from the tentative first person of the first article to an inclusive second person in his continued observations of the Zunis and their culture. Zuni was now a place in which he felt at home, and his comfortable berth at the governor's house gave him the foundation he needed for his next campaign, the assault on the pueblo's sacred spaces. By the end of the second piece, Cushing had been formally adopted into the family—the governor and his wife had given him his own "little house" (a smaller, sparer room in the household) and a Zuni name, Tenatsali, "Medicine Flower." He had successfully ferreted out the meanings of this private space, and, at the same time, used his foothold there to earn him entrance into related areas of the pueblo, those hinted at by the prayer plumes he had seen hidden in the rafters of the governor's house.[26]

Everyday effects were as important to salvage ethnologists as they were to those who followed them. Each scientist carefully detailed the processes of everyday life, and Cushing in particular applied the same painstaking historical analysis to the production of pottery as he did to Zuni mythology, and toward similar ends.[27] But the sacred practices of the Southwest's pre-industrial cultures held a special allure. Not only were the dances and costumes strikingly dramatic but they drew on carefully guarded secrets and so offered an irresistible challenge to these explorers. Furthermore, the apparently seamless bonding of spiritual with mundane life was in contrast to the liberal Protestantism of the ethnologists' own culture, which had, by the late nineteenth century, substituted a superficial sentimentalism for more powerful religious elements and to a large extent separated the spiritual and the material realms. So the kivas and shrines of Zuni, the pueblo's sacred places, exerted an almost metaphysical power over the scientists who came to enumerate and decode their secrets.[28]

The dramatic, animated figures of the kachina dancers represented only the most remarkable difference between the religion of Zuni and the liberal Protestantism of America's middle classes. The homogeneity of Zuni spiritual practices contrasted with the multiplicity that divided Protestants from one another, and from the Catholics, who were coming to the United States in increasing numbers (not to mention the Jews and the non-Christian Chinese at work on the rail lines that, by 1881, linked the Southwest to both coasts). Moreover, Zuni religion had a spatial dimension that both unified the pueblo and extended Zuni claims to areas and resources outside it that were vital to its spiritual and economic well-being. Cushing, the surveyor, cast a perceptive eye on these spaces, understanding that they held the key not only to Zuni cosmology but to the Zunis' ownership of the landscape. He had to be able to move through those spaces as freely as the Zunis did.[29]

Within the pueblo, the sacred spaces were easily evident, if not always easy to comprehend. The pueblo itself, its courtyards, passageways, and rooftops, was stage and gallery for the kachina dances that were the most public of Zuni's religious practices and that encompassed everyone in the pueblo as either participant or onlooker. This meant that, in effect, for brief periods during the cycle of the year the entire village was transformed into a sort of open-air cathedral. Just as there was no clear line between the Zuni men and the gods they impersonated, so there was no spatial division between sacred and secular, only a temporal one.[30]

Yet specifically sacred places did exist, hidden from sight except for the ladders protruding through the roofs. Each kachina society had a kiva, a windowless room in which its members prepared for their dances and other religious practices, built their altars, and held the secret portions of their ceremonies. The interdependent secret societies, each of which was concerned with a different aspect of the Zunis' physical, economic, and spiritual health, were the cornerstone of Zuni social cohesion. No single society could act in all realms. Membership in a given kachina society or fraternity depended on a complex set of relationships and circumstances, and each included members of various clans. Thus any family rivalries over secular issues would be mitigated by shared spiritual responsibilities. These guarded chambers contained the Zunis' most vital cultural secrets and the source of the pueblo's social stability.[31]

Dotting the landscape around Zuni were more ceremonial locations, secret caves, and shrines that figured in the cycle of rituals and dances that punctuated the Zuni year. These sacred places outside the pueblo fascinated ethnologists like Cushing and obviously distinguished Zuni religious practices from those of urban Americans. For some of the kachina ceremonies, dancers gathered at sites away from the pueblo that were connected with the mythological prehistory of the Zuni people. Then, costumed and impersonating their forebears, they would make their way into the pueblo, perform their dances there, and again disappear into the mythological landscape. Other sacred locations had economic as well as spiritual functions. The most important, the Zuni Salt Lake, sixty-two miles south of Zuni, provided the Zunis with salt and with a measure of income from other native peoples who desired the mineral. Sources for clay and turquoise were guarded secrets, and pilgrimages to any of these sites could be made only after the proper rituals.[32]

The restless and acquisitive Cushing was intrigued by all of Zuni's sacred places, but his first quarry lay within the walls of the town: the kivas of the secret societies. He might have used any number of approaches, including the threat implicit in being an agent of the politically and militarily powerful United States, a threat he was capable of making, as he had at Oraibi. But at Zuni, having insinuated himself into the governor's household and pleased at being able to operate as an insider, he negotiated his access in masculine games of bluff and bravado that seemed to be familiar to the Zunis. The games were subtle, and we have only Cushing's version of the story with which to analyze them. But his accounts of gradually pushing back the barriers with which the Zunis protected their ceremonies and kivas reveals a two-sided negotiation in which first Cushing, then his Zuni hosts, had the upper hand. The Zunis would set limits to his access, especially when he was sketching. Cushing would transgress them, the Zunis would threaten, Cushing would threaten back, and new boundaries would be set, to be negotiated anew at the next ceremony or secret meeting.[33]

To gain access to the ceremonies and permission to sketch, Cushing relied primarily on this pattern of threat and counterthreat, though he bettered his odds by insinuating himself into Zuni social life, living in the governor's house, and befriending the pueblo's women and children. His quest to enter and explore the kivas, however, took a slightly different form. This was more transgressive, he knew, defying the rules that kept away not only him but Zunis who were not members of the fraternities. But he succeeded with a strategy developed after paying careful attention to conversations he overheard and conventions he was allowed to witness. He first entered one of the secret rooms that he was so curious about by following the Koyemshi clowns (the mudheads he later impersonated for those photographs at the Smithsonian) back from a ceremony. He had gotten an invitation from a member of the group by offering to bring a present of candles and tobacco. The messenger who brought the invitation briefed him on what to say and warned him that if he forgot and spoke Spanish, which was forbidden, he should hold out his hands and feet to be struck with yucca wands. Cushing followed the instructions well, and when he lapsed into Spanish he withstood his punishment. He was hustled out of the room, but he had seen it and now left it as someone who had done more than observe.[34]

Later, learning that the Rattlesnake Fraternity lacked the black paint its members needed for an initiation ceremony, he bartered his own supplies of India ink to gain entrance to their meeting. He appeared in their chamber, descending the ladder "with perfect assurance," which excited those who were present. "Had a ghost appeared in their midst," he wrote, "he would not have caused more surprise than [did] my assurance and seeming familiarity with the forms." He made a loan of the ink and then withdrew respectfully, allaying some of the Zunis' fears. But then he returned to retrieve the ink, to which he ascribed almost mystical value. This time, he seated himself and stayed, despite protests from members of the group. He endured another sort of initiation, forced to smoke some sort of cigarette all night until he began to have gentle hallucinations, but he was rewarded by being allowed to witness the ritual initiation of two new members of the kiva.[35]

Thereafter, Cushing found himself more welcome in the kivas. He had neatly created his own sort of initiation into Zuni's sacred life with gifts, especially the ink, that involved him directly in preparations for the ceremony. At the same time, he forced the Zunis to allow him to participate, to be one of them, by letting them thrash him with their yucca wands and by smoking at their behest. Having done that, they had in effect taken him into their tribe; having treated him like a member, they could not afterward easily deny him a place in their society. He had manipulated their ritual forms and carved for himself a niche at the very center of their spiritual world.

That world was mysterious, beautiful, and dramatic. With his first glimpse of the Koyemshi's kiva, Cushing could enumerate its furnishings and give his *Century* readers a catalog of altars, sacred effigies, medicine bowls, and dance masks. In all, the scene he observed in the brightly lit room elated him. "This little glimpse," he wrote, "revealed to me a mysterious life by which I had little dreamed I was surrounded." His experience in the Rattlesnake kiva encouraged even more evocations:

> They occupied one of the largest rooms in the town, along the walls of which were painted figures of the gods, among them a winged human monster with masked face, and a giant cornplant which reached from floor to ceiling and was grasped on either side by a mythologic being. Toward the western end of the room stood the altar, with attendant priests before, behind, and on either side of it. Above all was suspended a winged figure, like the painting on the wall. Between the altar and the blazing hearth were gathered the members, all of whom, save the women, were nearly nude; but elaborate devices in red, white, and yellow paint, representing serpents, suns, and stars, made them appear dressed in skin-fitting costumes.[36]

During Cushing's first quick visit to drop off the ink, the Zunis in the chamber were at work making paint and costumes. When he returned late that night, he was blinded by a bright light in the room; pretending not to understand the objections to his presence, he seated himself. The Zunis shrugged and eventually acquiesced to his attendance; he began to smoke the cigarettes they handed him. Made ill by them initially, in time he achieved "the dreamy pleasures of the smoker" and, so softened, he observed the dramatic ceremony that began at midnight. His description is of a fascinating nightmare hallucination: birdlike shrieks, the surreal painted figures of masked dancers, the wild gyrations of one dancer who thrashed those who haplessly fell asleep. When the initiation ritual commenced, fires and grease lamps illuminated the room and filled it with smoke. He heard music, "wilder, more mysterious and deafening than ever," and then witnessed the painful, frightening ordeal of two young initiates, who were forced to take embers glowing at the ends of pointed sticks into their mouths. Quiet finally came when daylight filtered in through the hole in the roof. From above, women handed in food, and, for everyone except the two boys, who were fed stinging hot chilies, the nightmarish ceremony ended in a happy feast.[37]

Descriptions like this, and those of firelit dance ceremonies in the pueblo's courts and houses, gave Cushing's narrative an exotic, emotional power. The rational voice of Cushing the scientific observer—measuring interiors, counting artifacts, reproducing the minute details of all that he observed—was present, but to it was added another tone. This litany of sacred objects seen in his first glimpse of the Koyemshi kiva was relatively lifeless, citing the room rather than its inhabitants. But his evocation of the Rattlesnake initiation was all life and noise, movement and sensation, firelight and smoke, dizzying cigarettes, frightening noises, disturbing humanlike creatures, exhausted sleeplessness, and the all too physical violence suffered by the young initiates. For all the scientific specificity of the earlier description, it was the latter that drew his readers into the Zunis' spiritual world, giving them a feel for the intense spirituality of the kivas' enclosed spaces.

That spiritual world, secret and separate from the outside world, could be glimpsed not only through Cushing's early articles but in a bit of performance that he orchestrated when, in 1882, he brought a small group of Zuni elders east to Massachusetts to see the Atlantic Ocean. Though the trip was ostensibly a spiritual pilgrimage for the Zunis who had welcomed Cushing into their tribe, it also served as a publicity stunt for Cushing and for anthropology, much as Stevenson's visit to Washington with We'wha several years later would. The trip, which took the form of a series of meetings that were like kiva gatherings—Indian circles—allowed Bostonians to play at being Indian as Cushing had, enjoying the secrecy, exclusivity, and romance of another way of life in the company of authentic tribe members. Curtis Hinsley has linked this fascination for magic circles with another popular pastime, the séance, as well as with activities like those of the Boy Scouts and the Girl Scouts. The pueblo kivas, he suggests, offered an especially rich variation.[38]

Cushing's success in penetrating the secrets of Zuni's kivas distinguished his career there in a way that no subsequent anthropologist could duplicate. He ultimately became a member of the Priesthood of the Bow, the society responsible for protecting Zuni from its enemies both physically, as warriors, and metaphysically, as priests. Doing the bidding of the rain priests, this priesthood was the only society whose members could enter the kivas of all the other fraternities, and in it lay the de facto governance of the pueblo; the civil governor with whom Cushing lived was primarily a mediator between Zuni and outsiders. Cushing could now claim a direct knowledge of Zuni ceremonial life, where later students of the culture had to rely more heavily on the knowledge of informants.

The kivas held the information Cushing needed to gain a comprehensive understanding of Zuni ritual. But as he became more familiar with the spiritual cosmos of Zuni, he discovered aspects of Zuni religion that drew the Zunis out into the countryside, and he was convinced that these held, among other things, the key to Zuni prehistory. In the course of his five years in the pueblo, he ventured out on a series of exploratory adventures in what might be called ethnological geography, drawing his maps, such as they were, on the basis of information he gleaned from Zuni myths and legends and from hints he could coax from knowledgeable Zunis. Then he set out to find a number of Zuni religious sites, both to expand his understanding of Zuni beliefs and to demystify some of their practices.

Closest to the pueblo were the mountain ledges, caves, and half-hidden places where Zunis periodically built wooden shrines or planted plumed prayer sticks. Unlike Christian shrines, which were permanent and protected sacred relics from the elements, some Zuni shrines, especially those of the war gods, were designed to weather and decay outside, in the elements. Prayer plumes were put in caves and planted on mountaintops; the war gods were subject to wind and sand and rain, and new shrines were built elsewhere. These sacred caves and shrines in the land around Zuni were immediately interesting to ethnologists like Cushing, since they contained objects that, given a little secrecy, could be picked up like seashells and shipped back East.[39]

In a thinly fictionalized (and unpublished) piece entitled "The Treasure Cave of the Little Fire," Stewart Culin, a friend and admirer of Cushing, recounted one of Cushing's explorations, which was framed as a story of Culin's own efforts to uncover carefully guarded secrets:

> I bethought myself of the methods others had employed in making such discoveries. I recalled the story Tenatsali [as the Zunis called Cushing] told me of finding by means of clairvoyance the treasure cave of the Little Fire society. To be sure when as he believed escaping watching eyes he went by night to the cave and removed its contents piece by piece, the Indians who had followed him in secret made him put all back and never was he able to find the place again.

The claim of clairvoyance fits both Cushing's penchant for mystifying his talents and the romantic pleasure Culin took in believing that his friend had extraordinary powers. Cushing was not clairvoyant, but he listened closely to Zuni stories and inferred from them the essential clues for navigating the terrain the Zunis hoped to keep hidden from him.[40]

Cushing used his talent for interpreting narratives and separating the concrete from the purely imaginative with particular genius when he moved across the terrain around Zuni. Zuni culture reached far into the surrounding countryside, laying claim not only to natural resources but to sites that were significant to its history and religion. Their location was generally a well-protected secret, and access even to those that were not hidden was limited by tradition, taboo, and the presence of determined guards. Cushing listened carefully to the stories about these places, either informally or as part of ceremonial recitations, then compared them with information he received from traders and travelers who passed by, piecing together in ingenious ways maps of Zuni's ethnological geography. If Stewart Culin was correct, this is how he found the Cave of the Little Fire, and on the basis of such careful and intuitive reconstructions he also planned one of his more remarkable adventures.

Shortly after he had settled in the pueblo, in December 1879, Cushing undertook a journey to the northeast of Zuni in search of what he believed to be secret Zuni turquoise and jade mines. He had heard hints of the existence of such mines in the Zuni Mountains here and there as he talked with the Zunis. The information was enough to convince a prospector who happened through the area that he had in fact seen these mines; within a few days he, Cushing, and a third man, a wanderer, were on their way into the mountains. The trip, which Cushing described in his diary, in a series of letters, and years later with some embellishment in a newspaper interview, involved camping out in the snow and making stopovers at the home of a Mormon bishop and at a mining cabin. Along the way, Cushing explored the ruins of several pueblos. In time, his companions made off with the rope he used to secure his mule, which led to the loss of the mule and to a long, cold, apparently life-threatening walk back to the pueblo, though again Cushing was the guest of kind residents and was not so alarmed by his condition that he did not stop to investigate still more ruins. And though by his own account he was in terrible shape when he finally returned to Zuni, he pulled himself together and launched a second expedition within days, determined to complete the explorations that his misadventure with the mule had cut short. The second adventure was a success: Cushing located the mines, which proved to be the source not of turquoise and jade but of soft green and blue minerals the Zunis used for paint. He also thwarted the Zuni authorities who sought to limit knowledge of the site, at the same time impressing them with his fortitude and his uncanny ability to learn their secrets.[41]

What Cushing could do with the location of resources, he could also do with Zuni's veiled ancestral past. Perhaps the most fascinating aspect of Cushing's ethnological writings is his faith that the prehistory of the Zunis, and by extension of mankind in general, could be derived from oral traditions. All the ethnologists who worked at Zuni carefully cataloged the details of life and ritual they observed there, following standards set by John Wesley Powell for compiling vocabularies and grammars. But Cushing pressed the idea of the lexicon harder than the rest. He believed that careful classification and analysis of the language, and of the Zunis' decorative traditions, would reveal cultural survivals of an earlier age. As he had followed the clues of the incongruous mudheads to the theory of ancestors from the Lower Colorado River, so he attempted to re-create the prehistory embedded in these other Zuni artifacts.

Frank Cushing used the material culture and oral traditions of the Zunis to make new kinds of maps. From language and from artifacts, notably pottery, he deduced the progress of the Zunis' ancestors from their earliest beginnings to their present position on Lewis Henry Morgan's scale of civilization. His 1882 essay on Zuni pottery, for example, detailed what he presumed was the sequence of development in the art form and what historical events might have provoked each change in substance or style. From references in Zuni creation myths and the linguistic roots of modern Zuni words for water vessels, Cushing deduced that the earliest such receptacles were made of wood or cane. In time, they were replaced by gourds, which, when used to carry water, bore a name linguistically related to the word for cane. The gourds were in time encased in woven nets, which in turn evolved into woven baskets caulked with pitch to hold fluids. Baskets were lined with clay for cooking, which taught the Zunis' ancestors the benefits of firing: over time, clay pots were made on the model of baskets, which persisted only as decorative motifs on the surface of the pottery.[42]

In like manner, Cushing found rational sources for other Zuni designs that had accrued mythologies of their own over time. He deconstructed the pueblo's tradition of leaving the decorative lines around pots open, starting by questioning potters about the meaning of the practice: "They replied that to close them was *a'k ta ne*, 'fearful!'—that this little space through the line or zone on a vessel was the 'exit trail for life or being,' *o'ne yathl kwai na*, and that was all." Pursuing the question further, he learned that the Zunis assigned a sort of animate existence to their pottery, based, he thought, on the similarity between the sounds that pots made, particularly when they broke, and the sounds of human voices. This, combined with traditions that derived from the vessels' use in carrying water—"the source of continued life," he claimed—was why the Zunis thought of their pottery as animated and felt the need to leave a decorative exit trail.[43]

He was convinced, though, that the motif must also have had more practical origins. Having experimented with potting in order to learn more about its methods and its history, he came up with quite a simple explanation: it is harder to complete an incised or raised line on a pot than it is to leave it open. As potters developed new methods for decorating their wares with paint rather than with clay, Cushing reasoned, they continued the practice of leaving spaces in imitation of the earlier methods. In time, he argued, citing the British anthropologist E. B. Tylor, a "myth of observation" came to be associated with the practice.[44]

What Cushing did when he read deeply into Zuni pottery traditions was similar and complementary to what he did when he read the Zuni landscape, present and archaeological, and Zuni myths and legends. From all these sources, he deduced an explanation of who the Zunis were and how their culture had evolved. In the end, though there was more adventure in his telling, his story of Zuni hewed fairly close to the evolutionary narrative that guided Matilda Stevenson—it was a tale of savage tribes meeting barbarian ones, settling in, and developing over time both more sophisticated practical arts and organizational ones. This was a piece of the larger narrative, and despite Cushing's genuine respect for the Zunis it was marked by a tone that could be quite patronizing.

Cushing's account of Zuni gained much of its power from his narrative style, which transformed his anthropological work into an ongoing adventure. Essential to it was the presence of Cushing himself; just as his body was the center of his exhibits, so his mind relived the Zuni past. Cushing believed that he could think and act like a Zuni, and out of that thinking and acting came his explanations of the pueblo's history and culture. So in virtually every part of his narrative there was, in scientific garb, a sort of shape-shifting, of becoming Zuni while remaining himself. He demonstrated to his readers the capacity of civilized man to recover, almost physically, his ancestral past. He brought that past first into himself and then into his anthropological tracts and exhibits.

Cushing's ability to stand in for his subjects was a double-edged sword. It made him an empathetic observer and, combined with his talents as a storyteller, gave his descriptions of Zuni more life than Matilda Stevenson's weighty volume had, and, though they were shorter, more of a sense of comprehensiveness. He used his own experiences to smooth over the rough edges of his fragmentary evidence. In the service of his science, he moved fluidly from being scientist to being subject, exploiting both his powers as an outsider and his privileges as an insider at Zuni. But the boundary he trod there was dangerous, for his prestige as a scientist depended on his maintaining connections with a world that did not always approve of his adventures. His playing Indian could be, and was, read as heroic, but Matilda Stevenson thought him foolish, and accused him of wrapping his hair in curl papers at night to effect the native look he wanted to create; some of the officers at Fort Wingate found him uncouth rather than interesting when he appeared in his Indian garb.

A commitment to his science was one explanation for Cushing's willingness to walk on the edge between "civilization" and "savagery," but it did not belie his pleasure in sampling life on the wild side. In the late nineteenth century, as Gail Bederman has argued, manhood in the United States was being redefined, simultaneously rediscovering its connection with physical strength and claiming the superiority of its civilized refinement. President Theodore Roosevelt had famously transformed himself from a squeaky weakling into a burly hunter. Frank Cushing, whose biography bore some resemblance to Roosevelt's, was able, at Zuni, to express this two-sided, sometimes contradictory vision of manhood. As a scientist, he epitomized civilized behavior: rational, methodical, ruled not by passions but by intellect; as a Zuni, he could also express older forms of masculinity that seemed to have faded in the civilized world.

As Matilda Stevenson was able to use the access she was given thanks to We'wha's position between the two genders at Zuni, so Cushing was able to use his position between two types of masculinity. In large part, it was the disparity in social power that made this possible. For Cushing, Zuni, as a subject nation and as a representative of a less civilized race, was paradoxically a society of men who were simultaneously more and less masculine than himself. By the time he arrived at Zuni, it was a well-established convention to associate Native Americans, like other nonwhites, with femininity and subordination; the association between manhood and civilization, while undergoing redefinition, was secure. But since he ranked the Zunis below the level of civilization on the evolutionary scale, he could sample among them an older form of masculinity for which people like himself were powerfully nostalgic. Anthropologists like Cushing engaged with that anachronistic sense of manhood—the frontier cowboys-and-Indians sense—even as they drained it of its power.

At Zuni, when Cushing first arrived, there was still a class of men whose power stemmed from their prowess as warriors. Entrance into their fraternity came, according to Ruth Benedict, after lengthy purification rites that were deemed necessary when an enemy had been killed, so a prerequisite for membership was the capture of an enemy scalp.[45] Apaches and Navajos still raided the pueblo for horses and food periodically, and Zuni men, the agrarian, peaceful nature of their society notwithstanding, had the opportunity to act as warriors. Both because of his science and because he wanted to scale the gendered Zuni social hierarchy, Cushing set his sights on membership in this fraternity, the Priesthood of the Bow. He was determined to become a bow priest as the culmination of his experiments in participant observation. Having to produce an enemy scalp meant that he would have to find a way to mediate between the expectations of his own culture and those of his adopted culture, for a scalp was surely the most potent symbol of uncivilized behavior that existed in late-nineteenth-century America.

Cushing gained entrance into Zuni's governing council through dogged study and his insistence on being included, but also because he could mediate between Zuni and the United

States, helping to defuse situations that might otherwise have involved the Zunis with military authorities. He caused himself some trouble in Washington by helping them in a confrontation with Navajo horse thieves, and he was ultimately recalled by Powell when he interceded on behalf of the Zunis in a dispute over land (and water) with the son-in-law of a senator who threatened to cut Powell's appropriations. But his usefulness as an intermediary was not enough to overcome Zuni tradition: the bow priests insisted that he produce a scalp if he wanted to become a full member of the council.[46]

Cushing finessed the problem of the scalp with characteristic ingenuity, producing several different stories, all of which obscured the issue of how he had gotten the scalp. Altogether, he seems to have procured three scalps: two from existing collections in the East, one from his father, and the other apparently from the Smithsonian but possibly from someone in the army. Stewart Culin told one version of Cushing's story, presumably acquired through bits of information that he gleaned from whites near Zuni who had known Cushing or knew of him. In this version, Cushing perpetrated a droll hoax, riding out from the pueblo "debonairly on the war-path" only to conceal himself nearby to await the arrival of a scalp from the National Museum (the original acquisition of which Culin attributed to Lewis Henry Morgan, without, of course, suggesting that Morgan himself had taken it). Culin did not mention that the Zunis refused to admit Cushing on the strength of these secondhand scalps, so his wonderful short parable seemed to celebrate the civilized way in which any item might be acquired, and to hint at the strange power consumer goods had to blur differences between people—in this case the "savage" and the "civilized" man.[47]

Cushing himself was coy about the source for his scalps. In *My Adventures in Zuñi*, he wrote simply that he "strove for nearly two years to gain membership" in the esoteric society and "succeeded." Nearly a decade later, in 1890, he gave a more detailed account in a lecture on "Life in Zuñi," in which he described an arduous trip in the company of several Zunis to investigate the Havasupai tribe living in a branch of the Grand Canyon in Arizona. Returning, they encountered a group of Apache rustlers whom they eluded with a successfully executed subterfuge. Cushing, proud of his participation in this outsmarting of an enemy, admitted simultaneously that the Apaches "turned with the quickness of frightened game and scattered away among the bushes almost before we could fire a shot," and that he "returned from that expedition, at the end of a hot day, with a scalp, sole remaining requisite for my initiation into the Priesthood of the Bow, or the order of war magicians." Letters to Spencer Baird and the Boston journalist Sylvester Baxter, an enthusiastic publicizer of Cushing's work, were also vague as to the provenance of the scalp, burying the details in passive verbs. The raid "enabled me to secure a scalp," he wrote to Baird. To Baxter, he reported that "the scalps procured for me by my father and officers of the Army were insufficient in themselves for [admission to the Priesthood] . . . but the timely outbreak of the Apaches enabled me to acquire another and far more genuine article with right and title to possession."[48]

Did Cushing kill an Apache and take a scalp? Or did he somehow get the scalp without bloodying his hands? At least one historian, Jesse Green, has expressed serious doubts about Cushing's story of the raid. In any case, Cushing's studied vagueness would have protected both his claims to civilized behavior and his stance as a scientist, both of which were crucial to his relations with the Smithsonian director and the journalist, though the hint of savagery probably enhanced the romantic image Baxter had of Cushing. On the other hand, if he did not take the scalp, he petitioned for entrance into the Priesthood of the Bow under false pretenses, perpetrating another hoax on the Zunis, though possibly with their compliance. Either way, Cushing successfully negotiated between mutually exclusive ethical standards, managing to have it both ways.

For Cushing, adventures like these were central to ethnology, the source of both the detailed observations he was able to make about Zuni culture and the excitement that riveted him to it, despite real physical hardships. The Zunis transformed Cushing, in their own terms, from a "raw" outsider to a "cooked," finished Zuni. In the pueblo, he could be a man as he never could be in Washington or Boston, regardless of his status as an anthropologist or his popular notoriety. At Zuni Cushing could, with some safety (but also at real risk), indulge the fantasy of little boys and grown men playing at cowboys and Indians, exploring a sort of frontier of unmediated experience that civilization had pushed to the margins. The consumer culture that was creeping into every aspect of the day-to-day lives of more and more Americans had at its core an understanding that all experience could be packaged and sold, mediated by the marketplace. By the 1890s, simulated experiences, in crosscultural contact and in other dimensions, were available in the ingenious creations of carnival midways and amusement parks. Cushing's experiences at Zuni were rawer than these later abstractions, but they were of much the same quality.[49]

Becoming a Zuni warrior, Cushing became a man, making the passage through an initiation ritual that had no parallel in his own culture. But in doing so he also became a woman, in the sense that Native Americans and women were metaphorically associated in his culture; and being an anthropologist doubled that association, since it involved him in activities that often required more feminine than masculine attributes. Gaining access to the pueblo in the first place required that he woo its women and children. Creating a comprehensive ethnological description of Zuni required that he concern himself with domestic arrangements and social relationships; even his more dramatic insights into Zuni ceremonial life rested on the kind of work many women do, sitting still for long hours under difficult conditions, listening to the recitations of his informants, observing, and sketching while remaining for the most part in the background. And Cushing explored the world of women even more intimately. Pottery, after all, was an occupation of women, and when he took it up he transformed himself, temporarily, into a Zuni woman and her prehistoric ancestors.[50]

The practice of re-creating the process of cultural evolution, as Cushing did with pottery, was not, like some of his other speculations, unusual among ethnologists. If, as Lewis Henry Morgan maintained, all societies pass sequentially through the same stages of development, arriving at identical cultural forms, then the study of any one society at any given stage of development allowed anthropologists to generalize about all other societies at the same stage. And the psychic unity governing the pattern of development in turn allowed contemporary members of a "civilized" society to re-create the evolution in thought processes through which cultural practices emerge. Given the environmental conditions and technical knowledge available to so-called primitive peoples, living or prehistoric, Cushing was confident that he could replicate the processes through which their material and metaphysical worlds matured. When he sat down with Zuni women to make pottery, he willed himself to confront the problems of carrying water and preparing food as the Zunis and their ancestors did—first when they had only baskets, then when they discovered the properties of clay and the transformative capacity of fire. Working with Zuni's potters, he was simultaneously scientist and craftswoman, modern and ancient, American and Zuni, white-skinned and dark, masculine and feminine.

It was this kind of scientifically framed magic that made Cushing's Zuni story so attractive. Cushing was both a wily invader and a shape-shifter, and the Zuni world he conjured up as background for his adventures was designed to highlight his prowess. His scientific and technological expertise enabled him to outwit the dangers of an alien world by drawing on the advances of his own culture. But that drama would have been incomplete without the Zunis' own magic. Even as he exposed its practical roots, Cushing exploited the spiritual world of the Zunis, the wonderful animated gods who populated the pueblo on special occasions, and the colorful, unalienated, pre-industrial assumptions of everyday life there. All of these he used as a lush, complicated theatrical set for his anthropological adventures.

Five

"BLUE BEARD'S CHAMBER":
STEWART CULIN

In 1905 Stewart Culin, the first curator of ethnology at the Brooklyn Institute of Arts and Sciences (now the Brooklyn Museum), opened a hall there devoted to the southwestern United States that had as its centerpiece his impressive Zuni collection. Even before his last visit to Zuni the year before, the collection included 6,500 pieces. Masks, kachina dolls, fetishes, games, and more mundane objects illustrated life in the pueblo, while items from Zuni shrines highlighted the pervasive nature of religion in the everyday life of Native Americans in general and in the life of Zunis in particular.[1]

Culin's exhibit was impressive not only for the scope of its collection but for the skill with which he mounted it. He included artifacts of both ancient and modern manufacture, as well as relics from the Spanish period, from the sixteenth to the early nineteenth century. In one case, mounted on a wall, Culin arrayed eighteen kachina masks, three animal fetishes, a clay ball, and a pot in neat rows, then, above them, a roof plan of the central Zuni town. Whether these objects were old, new, or had been commissioned by Culin, it was impossible to tell from the information in the catalog that he wrote for the exhibit. He mixed the three without comment, which gave an air of time-lessness to the display and to Zuni, though he then framed the display, literally, with two treasured columns from Zuni's Spanish mission church that suggested, intentionally or not, a contrast between the historical nature of Western society and the ahistorical quality of Zuni time.[2]

Culin's visual conceptualization of an "ethnographic present" was in keeping with mainstream practices in museums of his day. But though he shared the basic assumptions of evolutionary anthropology held by other curators, he was troubled by the way most ethnological materials were displayed, and, unlike many curators of his generation, he thought of himself not as a researcher who also arranged exhibits but as a curator who did research. There was growing debate among curators and museum trustees, but for the most part anthropologists still believed that museums should be libraries of artifacts, storage halls in which serious students could examine as many examples as possible of each kind of artifact. The broader public purposes of the museum took second place.[3]

Culin reversed these priorities. It was probably no coincidence that he found a comfortable berth in Brooklyn, whose museum coupled arts and sciences and where art predominated. He wanted to tell a scientific story, but he was concerned with the aesthetic as well as the practical meaning of the objects he collected, and he wanted them to communicate not just evolutionary or historical sequences but a feeling for another way of life. At Harvard University's Peabody Museum, he complained, visitors never got "any of the feeling of the land or the people. One is always in the Peabody Museum, looking at museum specimens." He wanted to transport his museum visitors out of Brooklyn and into the Southwest—a journey of the imagination that was impossible, he thought, in the older science museums.[4]

John Hillers took this photograph of the pueblo in 1879. Much of the life of Zuni was carried out on the rooftops. Note the walled fields outside the pueblo and the broad, flat plain surrounding it. Ceremonial dancers often traveled across this expanse as part of their rituals. *Courtesy National Anthropological Archives, Smithsonian Institution*

This photograph, also taken by Hillers in 1879, is of the Zuni governor's house, probably the one Frank Cushing moved into soon after Hillers and the others left the pueblo. *Courtesy National Anthropological Archives, Smithsonian Institution*

This is a gentler view of Matilda Stevenson than sometimes circulated in Washington. *Courtesy National Anthropological Archives, Smithsonian Institution*

This caricature of Matilda Stevenson and her husband ran in the *Illustrated Police News*. The umbrella she wields is in a wry way a perfect symbol of the Anglo-Saxon civilization that gave her the confidence to take on the "savages" she met in the Southwest. *Courtesy National Anthropological Archives, Smithsonian Institution*

(*opposite, top*) Like Frank Cushing, We'wha reproduced Zuni forms in a Washington museum. We'wha demonstrated weaving techniques and donated some of what she wove to the National Museum. *Courtesy National Anthropological Archives, Smithsonian Institution*

(*opposite, bottom*) Using another typical Zuni loom, We'wha worked on a belt while exhibiting a fancy, perhaps ceremonial version of the dress, jewelry, and hairstyle Zuni women might wear. *Courtesy National Anthropological Archives, Smithsonian Institution*

Though Frank Cushing's costume was made up of Zuni materials, it was apparently his own unique design. His stance in this photograph resembles the one he adopted when Thomas Eakins painted his portrait. *Courtesy National Anthropological Archives, Smithsonian Institution*

Stewart Culin was never as comfortable in Native American dress as his friend Cushing, though he once wore Cushing's Zuni costume to a party at the Salamugundi Club in New York. *Courtesy National Anthropological Archives, Smithsonian Institution*

This photograph of a Zuni shrine, taken by Matilda Stevenson, nicely captures a difference in interpretation that was vital to salvage ethnology: to the Zunis, these were offerings to the gods; to the ethnologists, the shrine looked like a pile of discarded old things that, if they did not intercede, the elements would destroy. *Courtesy National Anthropological Archives, Smithsonian Institution*

Culin also wanted to distance his exhibits from older ones modeled on European ideas. He and Frank Cushing discussed his ideas about museum display in letters that followed their meeting at the Chicago World's Fair in 1893, when they began a very close, if brief, friendship. Culin believed that European museums were too encumbered with history, that the objects in them were overwhelmed by all the historical, literary, and aesthetic information that accompanied them. "The difficulty with the old sort of thing," Cushing replied, "which you need not fear will fail to be the old within a decade, is that it holds to the Cabinet literary and artistic idea, too strongly. This is because Museums originated in Cabinets, and in the old world, where so much is historic and where, for that very reason, they could, except for Cabinet purposes, have well been done without." Culin and Cushing preferred a fresher presentation in which visitors could learn directly from the objects in front of them, not from the accumulated cultural baggage they carried through the door. "Ours is a new world," Cushing continued, "where things speak as in time primaeval, and our museums become books and Histories or should become so, for the History of Man in America, is, thank Heaven, a natural History and an unwritten one!"[5]

Though Culin thought his ideas about museum display were radical, they were more conventional than he cared to admit. He was so proud of his collection that he wanted to show as much of it as possible, so he risked repeating the storage-hall mistakes of other museums. What rescued his exhibits from the ranks of the ordinary was his attention to aesthetics. He tried to arrange the massed masks and dolls artistically, and he surrounded them with watercolor paintings of the Southwest by Herbert B. Judy, an artist from the Brooklyn Museum who had gone with him to New Mexico. He also included mannequins that he had commissioned to showcase the costumes. These were not quite the life groups he had at one time envisioned, having been much impressed with those he had seen as part of the extensive anthropological exhibits at the Chicago World's Fair, but they had a special quality. Frank Cushing, in pursuit of authenticity, had posed for the figures in his Zuni dance exhibit, but Culin eschewed that sort of role-playing. For him, authenticity lay not in the pose but in the face. He had Father Michael Dumarest, an acquaintance in the Southwest, make plaster casts of the head, limbs, and trunk of one of his interpreters, "Zuni Dick," on the basis of which he could construct a mannequin for a Zuni dance costume. He wanted it to look like a recognizable personality, someone whom anyone who had been to Zuni would know, even if few in Brooklyn could tell the difference.[6]

Culin intended to place his audience in the world in which the artifacts they gazed at had been created, so he insisted on this bit of realism. To further facilitate the journey to that world, he created a mediating personality. Having earlier focused almost exclusively on collecting objects, he had little firsthand analytical material of his own; he himself had first seen Zuni through the eyes of Frank Cushing, and Cushing remained the primary source of his understanding of Zuni culture. For this reason, partly in tribute and partly as a literary device, Frank Cushing became the center of Culin's first Zuni exhibit.

The exhibit had two eye-catching focal points, neither of which featured the pure object that Culin was so sure could tell its story. One was a life-size mannequin of a Navajo medicine man clad in a costume that Culin had commissioned. (There may also have been the dancer mannequin based on Zuni Dick.) The other was an enormous full-length portrait of Frank Hamilton Cushing by Thomas Eakins. In this remarkable painting, Cushing, gazing down contemplatively on its viewers, stands in three-quarter profile, arms folded in front of him, hands grasping Zuni feathered prayer sticks. Behind him, an adobe pueblo wall shows various Zuni artifacts, including a shield painted in the distinctive geometric shapes used by tribes of the Southwest and hung heavy with feathers. To one side, a Zuni earthenware pot sits on top of an adobe oven. Cushing is wearing a costume that he assembled for himself out of Zuni elements: a headband wreathes his shoulder-length hair, an earring graces his ear, while a dark shirt, soft leather boots, and leggings decorated with silver studs mark him as an icon of the American West. He is identified with a society of Native Americans, yet not for a moment does he conceal his ancestry among the European conquerors of the continent.

It was perhaps too much to expect Brooklynites to feel like Indians—Culin himself could not make that imaginative leap—but he and they could imagine being Frank Cushing, standing confidently within the pueblo while at the same time remaining aloof. Eakins's portrait in the Brooklyn Museum made manifest the truth that anthropological exhibits were as much about anthropologists (and those who wanted to imagine themselves as anthropologists) as they were about Native Americans and Native American cultures. With the striking portrait of Cushing, Culin created a dramatic tableau of anthropological adventuring that could match the living tableau Matilda Stevenson had helped to choreograph at the kermis in Washington in 1886. The objects were important, but Cushing was the key. Visitors could join him and Culin in the challenge of puzzling out the meaning of objects, in the fun of imagining just how the odd tools were used or what spectacle emerged by firelight when the Zunis donned those inert masks, played those silent instruments, cooked and ate strange foods from this strange kitchenware.

Eakins's portrait evoked the dangers and adventures Cushing had written about, and museumgoers safe in Brooklyn could experience them vicariously. For those who had not read Cushing's own work, the press offered digests. A notice in *The Evening Post* the day before the exhibit opened enumerated the objects on display, drew attention briefly to the history of Zuni, and noted that "this village and region were first opened up by the great explorer and friend of the Indians, Frank Hamilton Cushing." A review in *The Brooklyn Daily Eagle* two days later also mentioned adventures behind the scenes. Predicting that the exhibit would place the Brooklyn Museum among the ranks of the best museums in the world, the reporter explained that "the museum's emissaries penetrated the heart of Arizona and New Mexico, into the little Indian villages, miles removed from any railroad. Remaining there for months at a time, they worked away to accomplish the object of their mission." He went on to specify the exact number of miles covered—8,829 in 1903 and 10,783 in 1904—"much of it afoot and on horseback." As for Cushing, "he lived among [the Zunis] for some time, as the first white man ever admitted to their number," and as to Culin's own adventures:

> It appears that the Brooklyn scientists had some difficulty in getting their material. It is against the native law to sell any article in any way connected with a religious rite, and when the strangers came to Zuni, the chief of the tribe, suspecting the object of their mission, sent a crier through the town, warning the inhabitants against bartering with the strangers under pain of immediate as well as eternal punishment. But some of the Indians were willing to take chances. They waylaid the members of the expedition at night and secretly conducted them to their shrines. In this way the museum secured many of the masks, "sacred cigarettes," and other material used in religious observances, interesting enough in itself, but doubly interesting once the beholder has a partial understanding of its deep symbolic meaning.[7]

The objects in Culin's exhibit, duly noticed, were given heightened interest by these reports on the danger and hardships of collecting. The newspaper report also drew attention to Her-

bert Judy's watercolors, which, the reporter suggested, "reproduce accurately and interestingly bits of landscape and architecture, as well as those larger phases of the native life that the
collection cannot reproduce as a whole. The pictures supplement the work of the collector in an attractive way, and will add
much to the popularity of Ethnology Hall." Culin did love the
objects in and of themselves, but they alone did not tell his story
as much as he believed they did. The other narratives of collecting and adventure, and Judy's contextual pictures, were vital to
his ethnological hall. In fact, the objects he had collected vividly
illustrated a story that he himself had carried into the field. He
had gone to Zuni with Cushing's accounts and the premises
of evolutionary anthropology as the scaffold along which he arranged his own story and the artifacts he collected. With the exhibit in Brooklyn, he skillfully integrated these various narratives
together with some from Zuni; his wonderful multimedia exhibit
told the story as he wished it to be known.

The Zuni that Stewart Culin imagined, through and around
his friend Frank Cushing, was a romance. He gathered the whole
into a three-dimensional visual narrative, with watercolor back-
drops, costumed figures, alluring props, and a larger-than-life
hero. By the time Zuni came to Brooklyn, it was the story not of
the pueblo but of Cushing in the pueblo and, by extension, of
Americans in the Southwest.

Frank Cushing wanted to re-create lost patterns of thought,
and Matilda Stevenson wanted to record what she thought were
the dying social practices of a doomed people. Stewart Culin
made objects themselves the primary focus of his concern.
Though by 1892 he could call himself an ethnologist, he never
did anthropological fieldwork as Cushing and Stevenson did.
Culin's passion was collecting, and what fieldwork he did was
generally related to explaining or authenticating the objects he
amassed. Though he did write a lengthy, cataloglike study enti-

tled *Games of the North American Indians*, which was published in 1907, his preferred medium was not print but exhibits.[8]

Stewart Culin, the son of a Philadelphia merchant, was born, like Cushing, in 1858. He joined his father's company after graduating from high school and gradually made a name for himself in the city, as both a relatively successful merchant and as an amateur ethnologist. He abandoned his mercantile career in 1892, when work at the museum of the University of Pennsylvania, where he was on the board, became extensive enough to engage him full-time, though he maintained an enthusiastic vision of the role of commerce and consumption in American society. He left few records of his business life, but his first foray into ethnology seems to have grown out of a collection of games he made. By the late 1880s, his interest in the origin and meaning of Chinese games—along with business responsibilities, possibly—had drawn him into a quasi-scientific study of Philadelphia's Chinese immigrant community. He kept an extensive scrapbook of printed notices about it and went to Chinatown himself to learn about mah-jongg, Chinese herbal medicine, and other aspects of Chinese immigrant culture.[9]

Striking what we can see as the keynote of early professional anthropology in the United States, Culin later recollected that when he came to ethnology he eschewed secondhand formal education for firsthand experience. In 1924, he wrote: "I might have gone to school and taken lessons from a professor. Instead I went to live in one of our Chinese settlements, where in time I came not only to speak the language but, eager and curious, saturated myself with the spirit of these interesting and capable people. It was the direct road to what I wanted to accomplish and I acquired a knowledge of the Chinese that has lasted with me to this day." Culin's mastery of the Chinese was less thorough than this suggests, just as his later ethnological work among Native Americans was relatively superficial, but his willingness to immerse himself in an unfamiliar culture and to try out another way of doing things put him, in spirit, in the company of ethnologists like Cushing and Stevenson, who were shaping the new profession.[10]

Because he had little formal education, Culin had to create his own professional credentials. Like Stevenson, he relied on early publications to establish himself as a serious student with privileged access to unusual and hard-to-come-by information; like Cushing, he allowed his exploits—having a Chinese pharmacist treat his cold, for example—to invest his experiences with added authority. His field was not yet Zuni but Philadelphia, and the city had plenty of associations in which an amateur could prove his seriousness. Culin immersed himself in Philadelphia's lively intellectual circle and joined an impressive number of its clubs and societies. Since the line between amateur and professional was as yet unfixed, Culin's participation in the Oriental Club, the American Folk-Lore Society, and the American Anthropological Association, which he helped found, went far in establishing him as a member of the scientific community.[11]

Culin made important friends in these associations, most notably Daniel Brinton, who, though a medical doctor by training, became the first university professor of anthropology and one of the United States' most distinguished anthropologists in the late nineteenth century. Culin and Brinton both joined the Board of Managers of the University of Pennsylvania's museum in 1890, and for Culin this was the start of a career as a professional ethnological curator. By 1892, he was devoting himself to the museum full-time, creating exhibits for two expositions commemorating Columbus's voyage, one in Madrid and one in Chicago.

In Chicago, Culin won a gold medal for his folklore exhibit, which combined evolutionary principles with popular tastes; his subject—toys, games, and charms—struck a chord with the public that was simultaneously familiar and exotic. It also interested

Frank Cushing, who, with William Henry Holmes, had assembled an impressive and innovative exhibit featuring life-size figures dressed and posed as if they were engaged in a Zuni ceremonial dance. Culin and Cushing discovered a mutual interest in the evolution of games, sharing a belief that those of Asia (Culin's specialty) bore more than coincidental resemblance to those of North American natives. The two men made plans to write a study together about the relationship between the two continents. Cushing, who died seven years later, never wrote his portion, but Culin was so drawn to the subject that he pursued it among Native Americans and wrote a comprehensive study.

Culin's almost single-minded concentration on Native Americans began after Cushing's death in 1900, spurred in part by a sense of obligation to complete Cushing's work as a memorial. He ventured westward on behalf of the University Museum for the first time in 1900, financed by the Philadelphia department-store magnate John Wanamaker. It was a whirlwind collecting tour on which he joined his friend George Dorsey, an anthropologist and a curator of the Field Museum in Chicago. He made more trips for the museum in 1901 and 1902, and built an impressive collection in quite a short time.

It was during his 1902 expedition that he first visited Zuni, an experience that was part buying trip and part pilgrimage:

> It was with no little emotion that I first looked on the town, rising like a huge ant hill above the plain, with smoke from the evening fires hanging low over the house tops. Zuni was at last a reality. No longer vague and far away, the center of a world of fancy which the genius of my dear friend Cushing had created, but a solid substantial Indian town, with men and women swathed in scarlet blankets moving here and there on the outskirts of the settlement.

This first trip was only a brief introduction to that "solid, substantial Indian town." Culin had some trouble getting an interpreter, because he had arrived when the Zunis were preparing for a dance ceremony. He tried to find people who would sell him artifacts, particularly kachina dolls and dance masks, but he was still an outsider and had not yet discovered how to buy what was not available for sale. For the most part, he contented himself with exploring some of the shrines outside the pueblo and with observing, in some detail, the elaborate costumed dances that were taking place in Zuni's courtyards, dances that included performances by a fraternity that swallowed small tree trunks the way sword-swallowers swallowed swords.[12]

On this trip, Culin was not as successful in acquiring artifacts as he was on subsequent visits, but his expedition report and a memoir written two decades later establish the eclectic tone that distinguishes his Zuni work. He was very serious and methodical as a collector, and when he made ethnological observations, as he did at the tree-swallowing dance, his notes were precise and detailed. Yet for all his concern for accuracy, he apparently made no effort to find out from participants or other observers what this dance meant or what it was supposed to accomplish. His expedition report reveals no such information and gives no indication that he was curious. What was observable was what was important.

On the other hand, in other writing, distinct from his reports, he indulged a far less scientific imagination. In a brief essay on "Zuñi Pictures," which Elsie Clews Parsons included in her 1922 anthology *American Indian Life*, Culin reconfigured his 1902 report with an eye to a more popular audience. In this brief prose snapshot, Culin gave free rein to a side of his personality that he kept out of his professional expedition reports but that found expression in brief essays like this and in some rather poor unpublished short stories. The body of the essay included details about his trip and the dance he witnessed, much abbreviated, and he embellished the account with bits of local color; overall, this rendition was folksier, giving the impression of a wide-eyed Culin quite different from the shrewd professional collector of the reports.

"If there was any one thing in the wide world I wanted to do more than another," he wrote, "it was to visit the New Mexican pueblo where my friend Tenatsali spent so many years of his strange career. He had discovered it and made it his own and before his death he turned over to me his title to its romance and mystery." With this opening, Culin made it explicit that his 1902 trip had been a pilgrimage inspired by Cushing, and made it seem all the more exotic and authentic by referring to his friend only by his Zuni name, Tenatsali. Culin had come to Zuni, by this account, to claim a strange legacy, not, as one might suppose, the scientific legacy of an early anthropologist but the romance and mystery of another society. Cushing existed here as a Zuni and not as a Zuni—a note at the bottom of the page revealed his name—yet Culin stressed Cushing's Zuni identity and gave him the unqualified distinction of having discovered the pueblo "and made it his own."[13]

The businesslike tone of the earlier report was replaced by a low-key anecdotal air. Culin suggested that the visit was an impetuous break from a cross-country trip: "It happened one winter while crossing the continent I heard there was to be a dance at the pueblo. The news decided me. I stopped off on the railroad, hired a team from the sheriff and had him drive me down to the town." His first stop was a stone house outside Zuni that Cushing had built when he lived at the pueblo. Cushing himself had never lived in the house, Culin reported. It had "dropped from his lavish hands" and was, when Culin arrived, a trading store run by a jovial farmer-agent. The agent invited Culin to stay with him, welcoming him "as an old friend," and Culin spent a cozy evening in front of the fire listening to the agent tell stories.[14]

The scene Culin conjured up for his first night at Zuni, near but not in the pueblo, recurred in his attempts at fiction: travelers, missionaries, traders, all strangers in the strange land of the Native Americans, gather together to tell one another tales in the comfortable, companionable glow of the fire. In one story, "Pictures of Travel," the fireside gathering gives form to an American West version of the *Decameron* or of *The Canterbury Tales*, in which each man tells a tale of the mystical happenings outside, and the warmth of the fire bonds the strangers against the eerie, supernatural power of the surrounding country. In "Zuñi Pictures," the trader's stories are about Cushing, and their memories of the ethnologist bind the men together.[15]

Of all the stories about Cushing that Culin might have heard, he chose to start with the one about Cushing's hiding out in the stone house while awaiting the arrival of the scalp from the National Museum, part of his attempt to join the Priesthood of the Bow. The tale seems an odd choice, given Culin's desire to claim Cushing as a Zuni, and yet perhaps it makes sense. It identifies Cushing, like Culin and the agent, as an outsider at Zuni, someone who has to seek refuge from the people among whom he lives. It also makes Cushing simultaneously a Zuni and better than a Zuni, capable of fooling his adopted people with a ruse and determined to play their game without sacrificing the higher moral imperatives of his own society.[16]

In the remainder of this brief essay, Culin recounted other episodes in his first trip to Zuni. He went hiking with a young boy to see shrines tucked among the steep sides of a mesa to the east, but he seemed, on this visit at least, more impressed with the agility of the barefoot boy in the snow than with the shrines they found. When they returned to the store, they found the sort of eclectic group that Culin included in his story cycle:

> There was Jesus, the Mexican, and French Dan, Falstaffian and dissolute. There was the Missionary whom later I was to know

better and the Field matron, a wraith of a woman who went silently among the Indians and gave them some drug she had discovered through an advertisement in the "boiler plate" of her home paper. There were the Indians who fraternize with the whites, like the Albino and the old Mormon, or to give him his full name, Ten Cent Mormon, because he had been baptized by the Mormons in the early days and received ten cents to bind the bargain.

This party had gathered because of the dance to be held in the pueblo. Part of the ritual of some of the public dances in the pueblo involved welcoming all visitors (though Mexicans and Navajos were sometimes excluded and demonized). Those who joined Culin and his host at dinner, including the sheriff who had driven Culin in, were fascinated by the prospect of the dance, which had not been performed for some time, and that fascination seemed to shade into something like belief in its powers. Like the tale-tellers Culin imagined in "Pictures of Travel," the agent and the sheriff seemed to Culin to be willing to accept Zuni claims to supernatural power. His tone in reporting this has the effect of opening it as a possibility rather than dismissing it as superstition.[17]

Culin was intrigued by the palpability of Zuni belief in the supernatural. He closed "Zuñi Pictures" with a description of the tree-swallowing dance that had figured prominently in his 1902 report, but the sober, scientific observation of the early version had given way to something more colorful. First, he set the stage for the drama: seated on a red blanket, he observed "every living soul in the pueblo, dressed in their best and gayest clothes," gathered on the rooftops to watch the dance in the courtyard; and the courtyard seemed to Culin a perfect theatrical setting, an enclosed space in the center, a "long, white, wooden box painted in colors with cloud-terrace and rain symbols," and passages on either side for the dancers. As the ceremony began, two men took up notched rattles and began to scrape them rhythmically with bits of sheep bone. "There are few more mysterious and disturbing sounds than this same scraping," Culin wrote suggestively. "The time is perfect, the rhythm inexorable. Something was about to happen."[18]

The scene that followed was indeed dramatic. Two processions of white-painted dancers entered, their heads thrown back and spruce trees sprouting from their open mouths. It was "a moving forest." Among them were women, one with a white mask that particularly interested Culin, and children, including "a tiny boy with a miniature spruce" who "brought up the rear." When everyone had entered the courtyard they stopped, silent. "The dancers rested, withdrew the trees from their mouths and held them, butts upward with the top boughs resting on the ground. Then it was that the full significance of the performance was revealed. The butts, rudely chopped to a tapering point eight or more inches in length, had been entirely swallowed."

At this point the "significance" for Culin was merely a sort of carnival trick. Yet as the music started up again and the dancers resumed their dance, he too was caught in the strange power of it all:

> Again the strident notes of the rattles sounded. The dancers took up their trees, elevated and adjusted them in their mouths and danced as before. There was the same volume of coördinated sounds, of gourd rattles, of resonant shells and the swish, swish of the garments. Again the white mask danced on. . . . It grew dark and I left the plaza, in a daze. What did it all mean— the painted box, the swallowed trees, the white mask?[19]

This and other rather mystical writings date from relatively late in Culin's career, for the most part after he had finished assembling his collections of Native American artifacts and was reconsidering their source from some distance in both space and time. His marriage in 1917 to Alice Mumford Roberts, a painter of sentimental pictures, may have influenced the shift in his perceptions of Native American societies, though by the 1910s and 1920s he had also begun to lean toward the arts mandate of the Brooklyn Museum and away from science, with the result that he had become more concerned with the spiritual meanings of his artifacts.

By and large, in his field reports Culin respected the seriousness of Zuni spiritual beliefs and practices, noting in his 1902 report "the reverence and propriety with which the ceremony [of the tree-swallowers] was conducted" and "the strong religious sense of the people." Indeed, he contrasted the "order and sobriety" of Zuni with the near-anarchy of the station town of Gallup, much to the credit of the Native Americans. At the same time, like his predecessors, he was frustrated by what he considered the silly superstitions of those who refused on spiritual grounds to sell him the artifacts he wanted.[20]

Culin was as passionate about collecting as Cushing was about becoming a bow priest. He thought in terms of complete sets and, more than Cushing and Stevenson, he epitomized the salvage ethnologist. He disparaged government attempts to ban ceremonial dances and other Indian customs. "Left to themselves," he wrote in 1902, "the dances and other native customs will go too soon—alas, for the student of aboriginal customs and religion." His response to this prognosis was to concentrate almost exclusively on the material culture of the fading societies, collecting sets of things that could, in the future, tell the story of the people who had disappeared. He liked the idea of making a full study of one tribe rather than of gathering bits and pieces from many tribes, and his attention fell on Zuni, the legacy Cushing had left him. The ethnological research he did revolved around ascertaining just what a complete set of Zuni artifacts might consist of. He was fascinated by the ancient, the historical, and the currently used manufactures of the tribe, and he set about discovering ways to purchase all of these, even if, as sometimes happened, obsolete or sacred items had to be manufactured specifically for his collection. Culin faced challenges to his quest for a comprehensive collection from the Zunis themselves, and from other anthropologists, notably Matilda Stevenson, whose sojourns in the pueblo overlapped his. But these challenges, as with both Cushing and Stevenson, served to heighten, not dampen, his interest.[21]

Unlike Cushing and Stevenson, Culin tended to play a secondary role in the drama of actually buying artifacts. He made only a few trips to the sacred places in the countryside surrounding Zuni, and always with others—Zuni guides or Andrew Vanderwagen, a trader who did the work of getting the artifacts. More often, he simply set up shop in the pueblo and invited people to sell him old things; the Zunis took to calling him I-no-tai—"Old Things." When he could get an interpreter to go with him, he sometimes traveled from house to house asking for things, but for the most part he depended on the power of cash to bring the artifacts to him. And he was remarkably successful.[22]

His first trip, in 1902, was merely an introduction. His report contained few references to collected articles, though he did acquire enough sacred objects to raise an alarm in the pueblo, and he learned that those who had sold him masks risked punishment:

> I was ultimately successful in purchasing nine masks, but shortly after my advent, a cryer was sent around, who called out to the people and cautioned them against selling me any masks, and I was told that the sale of masks was punished by death. In point of fact, a person who sold masks was likely to be whipped, there being a teniente (officer) who knew them all, and constantly made the round of the houses to see that none were missing.[23]

When he returned in 1903, conditions were more favorable for his purposes. The pueblo was largely deserted. Most of the men were still out in the farming districts to which they moved during the planting and harvesting seasons. Those who remained in the pueblo, primarily women and children, were very poor, and Culin offered them a sort of emergency relief. Word went out that he was staying with Andrew Vanderwagen, and that he wanted to buy things. There followed a procession of women and children "bringing the usual assortment of small rubbish," as well as some items, particularly sacred games, that he very much wanted but that were "surrounded by the same secrecy as the masks and other ceremonial appliances." The women, he wrote later, "brought me many things that the men would not sell, things which they had gathered in the dark inner rooms; things long disused, of which they did not know the significance or value."[24]

Even more exciting, for Culin, was a collection Vanderwagen had made for him during his absence. Vanderwagen himself was an interesting character. Originally a Protestant missionary, by 1902 he had given up religious work for the life of a trader. From the descriptions in Culin's expedition reports, he seems to have been a good-natured, hardworking family man with an exceptional entrepreneurial eye and a knack for ethnological collecting. Later, in his fiction, Culin referred to Vanderwagen as "the Missionary" (the same Missionary, no doubt, who appears among the crew gathered in the agent's house before the dance in "Zuñi Pictures"), and the characterization stresses his religious affiliation, suggesting that Vanderwagen ran his trading post as a sideline to support his mission, that he sold Zuni religious artifacts in part out of iconoclastic fervor and in part to raise money when mission funds were low. Culin also attributed to Vanderwagen a rather unchristian shrewdness: "As a missionary he was gentle, diffident and compassionate. As a trader, and I speak with knowledge for he sold me a horse that went lame in a week and had vices of which I had never heard, he could out-trade even and [sic] Indian, not to say a Mormon."[25]

Whatever Vanderwagen's true character, he was the source of several of Culin's most interesting adventures at Zuni. The collection he surprised Culin with in 1903 consisted not only of a large number of kachina dolls and dance masks that Culin had looked for unsuccessfully the year before but also of the "entire contents of three of the most ancient and sacred of the Zuñi shrines from the neighboring mountains." Vanderwagen had secreted the collection in his house, aware that it would raise considerable trouble if the Zunis learned of it. When Culin returned to a still largely deserted Zuni after a brief absence to lecture to a congregation of Mormons on the probable cultural connections between prehistoric Americans and Asians, he learned that a Zuni servant of Vanderwagen's had let in a group of Zunis, causing "great excitement." In anticipation that the council to be held that night would try to repatriate the artifacts, "the missionary determined to remove his collection from the town." Culin, discovering that he himself had business that needed immediate attention in Gallup, "offered to act as escort," and was "before dawn on my way to the railroad."[26]

Culin told this story in far more dramatic form in his later unpublished short fiction entitled "Blue Beard's Chamber." As is evident from the title, Vanderwagen emerges as more sinister, though in fact he ran a noisy household full of children, animals, and visitors that argued against his keeping any big secrets. In the short story, the narrator settles in with the missionary and begins to buy artifacts from the "wretchedly poor" Indians while the missionary carries on his trading business. The missionary allows him "full run of his establishment," including both an excellent library and a "rare luxury in the desert, a porcelain-lined bathtub," but he is warned against entering "one room in the warehouse, a kind of Blue Beard['s] chamber to which [the missionary] alone had the key."

The narrator gives little immediate thought to what might be in the locked room, busy as he is with a continuing procession of women during the day and men at night, often cloaked in secrecy, who brought him objects they hoped he would buy. He is disappointed by the offerings, for they rarely have, he says, "real utility or value." When younger tribal members start to manufacture "antiquities," he sees a way to acquire the sacred things he really wants, while at the same time giving an economic boost to the impoverished pueblo. He thinks he might commission what he needs, starting with secular objects, including a suit of clothes like the one Cushing wore, and working up, in time, to the masks that were forbidden him. The project is unsatisfactory: the clothes he wants are obsolete, and just obtaining the materials for the artisans is almost impossible. Even deerskin has to be imported from a department store in Denver, as game laws prohibit killing deer in the territories. The narrator, like Culin, does succeed in buying an old silver forge as well as "bellows, moulds [sic] and tools, everything in fact down to the cotton underclothes which the smith wore." But his experiment as a "patron of industry" proves him a "bungling amateur."[27]

The narrator continues to look at an unending number of items offered for sale. He finds them mostly useless, but, assured by the missionary that the nickel he is offering for each item represents "the sole support and stay of the community," he "could not leave them to starve" and so continues to fill up the warehouse. Despite his economic importance to the pueblo and a vague awareness of "mysterious comings and goings after night fall" at the missionary's house, which he associates "with the more esoteric work of the Mission," he decides to make a trip southward to a Mormon settlement. (He admires this "enterprising and thrifty community," and is tempted to stay and enjoy his "luxurious life in this well-watered town.") But then he has "a sudden impulse to return to the pueblo." When he gets back two days later, the missionary and his family are away and Lorenzo, their Indian servant, is "sullen and uncommunicative." The missionary returns, "pale and trembling," to report that Lorenzo showed the war chiefs what was in the locked chamber during his absence, and he nervously reveals the chamber's secret:

His story went back to my visit to the Pueblo the preceding winter. He had not spoken to me then, but had gathered my general purpose from what he overheard and set the Indians at work and provided hide, paint and feathers. "You never would have had the courage to do it yourself," he exclaimed. So this was the secret of those nightly conferences. "It was all for you I did it," he moaned. So this was the explanation of the carefully-locked room. There was no time to be lost. He led me to the warehouse, inserted the key and threw open the door of the forbidden chamber. There, hung from the rafters in mysterious array, were long rows of masks, each one more grotesque and terrifying than its neighbor. There were the long-beaked heads of the giants, beloved by the Navajo, and Siatosha with his projecting horn, the mud-bedaubed clowns and the many-spotted fire god. For a moment pride overcame his fear. "Are they not wonderful," he exclaimed. "Made with all the necessary prayers and fastings. I attended to everything. Now how much will you pay for them?"

Culin's narrator steps in to salvage the situation:

"Let us pack this stuff," I cried, "and get away!" The big wagon was loaded hastily by the Navajo teamster, piled [so] high that it cast a long shadow in the light of the rising moon. I saddled and looked for the missionary. "Hurry! Hurry!" "No!" he replied. I stay here with my own," and so I left him standing there alone in the moonlight.[28]

This is a far cry from the low-key way in which the adventure unfolded in Culin's expedition report of 1903. It suggests that Culin rather enjoyed his brief brush with tribal authority, and that he liked to imagine broader adventures than he actually had. In fact, the manufactured artifacts were delivered uneventfully to the rail station in Gallup, and Culin returned to the pueblo to attend a rain dance, which repopulated the pueblo. When it was over and people began to return to their farms, he resumed purchasing artifacts "in a quiet way" and then more openly. He and Vanderwagen traveled into the mountains and collected prayer plumes and other artifacts. He made two offhand references to the incident at Vanderwagen's, one to the effect that nobody offered him sacred objects "in consequence of the recent trouble," the other that "it was a common opinion in Zuñi that the sale of the dolls to Vanderwagen, the violations of the ancient shrine, and other acts of impiety, would result in drought and failure of the crops." If there were other consequences—to Vanderwagen's Zuni accomplices, for example—Culin did not pursue them.

By the time Culin returned in 1904, Vanderwagen had established something of a cottage industry in the manufacture of Zuni artifacts. He had purchased a ranch outside the pueblo and, in addition to sinking a well and making other improvements, had employed three Zunis to make masks and dolls to fill out Culin's collection; work on the well was a cover for the Zunis' manufacturing activities, and they worked through the winter in a locked room in the ranch house. Culin bought their entire output: it included fifty dolls, for which he paid four dollars apiece, to add to the seventy-three he had bought from Vanderwagen in 1903; twenty-four face masks at five dollars each; and eighteen pot-shaped masks for ten dollars apiece. For an even five hundred dollars, Culin was able to make his collection comprehensive, if not exactly "authentic," without dealing directly with the Zunis at all.[29]

Vanderwagen's enterprise occasioned no special notice from

the pueblo, perhaps because of his judicious use of subterfuge and his decision to move the manufacturing site away from the pueblo. Culin's description of the pueblo on this visit was of a more open, easier place than he had encountered in 1902 and 1903, though it is unclear whether that was due to a change in the Zunis or to his own growing familiarity with them and his association with Vanderwagen. No doubt it had something to do with the fact that Vanderwagen had, through his little factory and his forays into the hills to collect relics from older shrines, satisfied Culin's appetite for taboo objects, so that Culin spent his time wandering the pueblo in search of tools and other more mundane treasures. At the same time, Matilda Stevenson was also in the pueblo, finishing work on *The Zuñi Indians*, so there was some competition and even cooperation between the two as they vied for artifacts.

Culin's collecting adventures in 1904 also involved artifacts that were not specifically Zuni. His interest was now drawn to things that Cushing had brought to or used at Zuni—English bows and arrows, and a camp stool—and to relics of the Spanish period. The Catholic Church of Our Lady of Guadalupe, which was in a constant state of disrepair, had once contained four carved wooden columns commissioned by a Spanish missionary in the 1770s. Culin learned that the columns had been removed from the church by one of the village leaders, Gak-kwai-mo-si, and he began to pursue the possibility of purchasing them. The man was reluctant to sell at first, but under pressure from Culin he finally agreed to the price of a hundred dollars. Culin negotiated through the man's son and wife (or mother—Culin's language is a bit unclear here); though the family agreed to the sale, they feared that others in the pueblo would discover and disapprove of the transaction.[30] So Culin bided his time, traveling to the farming villages to buy farm tools, picking up the Cushing relics, and visiting Zuni houses in search of other artifacts.

Finally, on June 17, his Zuni interpreter, Nick Graham,

brought word that the negotiations had been completed. But the adventure had only just begun. The deal required that Culin take possession of the heavy columns in the dark of night. The boy and the old woman with whom he had bargained for the pieces agreed to let him in at one o'clock in the morning. Culin awaited the appointed hour in Vanderwagen's parlor with Herbert Judy, the artist from the Brooklyn Museum, who had come out to do sketches for Culin's exhibits. "At about eleven," Culin wrote, "the last light in the village was extinguished, and the dogs became quiet. We unlocked Vanderwagen's stable, and with some new wool sacks, started for the town shortly before one." They missed the house on their first try, though they alerted dogs all around them. When they finally found the right house, their signal, a tap on a window, brought no response. In the quiet night, Culin claimed to hear nothing but the sound of snoring, "loud, long drawn, and regular, that seemed to come from all the neighboring houses." Frustrated by his failure to gain the attention of his co-conspirators, he climbed the ladder to the roof, climbed down into the room where the family was sleeping, and roused the old woman. Culin retreated, and in time the door below silently opened for them, though Culin did not know who had opened it or who shoved the columns out to him.[31]

Culin and Judy then covered a column with two of the sacks they had brought with them and began the work of moving the unwieldy object. With much hard work, they managed to get it out of the village, through Vanderwagen's wire fence, and into the stable. The operation had taken them a full hour and had exhausted them. Culin counted out twenty-five dollars for the first column, gave it to the boy, and he and Judy turned in for the night. The next night Culin returned for the remaining three pillars, taking not only Herbert Judy but a Navajo teamster who sometimes worked for the Vanderwagens. With four men (the fourth was probably Nick Graham), the task went more quickly;

by 2:30 a.m. all four heavy timbers were safely in Vanderwagen's stable.

The adventure was not yet over, though. Culin dispatched the columns to Gallup, camouflaged beneath a load of hides and wool in the Vanderwagens' wagon, in care of the Navajo driver. Then he began to worry about his treasure. A Zuni who had gone partway with the wagon had peered under the hides and seen the columns but apparently didn't know what he was looking at. That crisis past, Culin learned that Matilda Stevenson had hired a team and set off for Gallup the next day. Culin was already suspicious of her, for the morning after he had secured the first column she had come calling, ostensibly in search of information about some other artifacts, a forge and an altar, that she had heard Culin might be trying to obtain. Culin feared she might hear of his purchase of the columns and did his best to draw her attention to other things. Wary of her intentions, Culin jumped to the conclusion that Stevenson planned somehow to expose his coup.

He listened carefully to all the gossip that reached him. "It is amazing," he wrote, how "news travels in this country, as well as the constant surveillance under which everyone is kept, and the knowledge everybody has of everybody else's business." Unable to convince himself that all was well, Culin himself headed for Gallup. At the Vanderwagen ranch he learned that Stevenson had in fact passed some time there, but that she had been on a quest that was completely unrelated to his shipment. Satisfied that Stevenson "was not on the track of the columns," Culin continued on to Gallup, passing Stevenson, with a load of boxes, on the way. When he reached Gallup the next day, he was relieved to find his columns safely stored in a basement, ready for shipment to Brooklyn. For all the excitement of the chase and his night ride, Culin's concern and interest ended once he knew that his possessions were secure. Without even starting a new sentence in his report, he moved on to another subject: a visit with someone in Gallup with whom he discussed labor conditions in Gallup and a mining strike there.[32]

For all the late nights and false alarms, this adventure turned out, like the adventure of the locked chamber, to be fairly tame. It was acquisition that excited Culin. He enjoyed, in his reports and in his fiction, demonstrating his mastery of the craft of obtaining rare objects and of outsmarting the Zunis and other anthropologists in getting them. But his detachment from the living world of those artifacts distinguishes him from Cushing and Stevenson. Nowhere in his account of his acquisition of the pillars does he mention any effort to find out their history or their current use and meaning for people in the pueblo, though they must have had considerable value if such subterfuge and hard work were required to remove them. Surely they must in time have been missed, and yet Culin lost interest once his mission was complete.

Culin made one more collecting trip to Zuni as part of an extensive tour of the Southwest in 1907. In Los Angeles, at a "so-called Indian Crafts Exhibition," he was struck by the poor quality of the crafts, which consisted partly of " 'souvenirs', and trinkets more or less suggestive of the Indians in their design or material, and of white manufacture," and partly of rather disappointing Indian crafts, many of which were "so poor and tawdry as to lead me to question whether Indian art has any decorative value." Culin had been critical of contemporary Indian crafts ever since his first visit to Zuni. The pressures of the market, for which an increasing portion of Indian crafts were destined even in 1902, had, he remarked, caused the quality of Zuni pottery and other crafts to deteriorate, as craftspeople adopted "numerous inartistic innovations . . . to supply a demand for novelties."[33]

Returning to Zuni in 1907, Culin encountered the market all around him. Zuni itself appeared to him much improved, infused with a "general air of prosperity" that surprised him. On the other hand, where he had always found someone at Zuni eager to lodge and feed him, this frontier custom seemed to have fallen into disuse. A doctor who had come to live at Zuni some years earlier was able to offer a room but no food; the storekeeper, likewise, could not provide him with a meal. The missionary who had taken Vanderwagen's post in the pueblo was away, and Culin was told that he would not give food or shelter to visitors. Having tried the non-Zuni residents, Culin turned to his Zuni interpreter, Nick Graham, who was now the proprietor of a well-kept store. Nick prevailed upon his wife to cook some eggs Culin had brought, and Culin at last had "an excellent supper, served on a table with a cloth, with silver spoons and good, clean, china." This Zuni, at least, had adopted American habits while retaining Zuni standards of good manners when it came to enter-taining visitors.[34]

The prosperity of Zuni in 1907 may have been the result of good weather conditions. Culin remarked on the "vivid green" of the pueblo gardens. But the pueblo had also become a lively crossroads. Staying, eventually, at the Vanderwagens' ranch, which he had hoped would be quieter than the pueblo and a bet-ter place to "work with the Indians," Culin encountered a virtual parade of people who stopped at the ranch and paid ten cents to water their horses. "The people are of various sorts," he wrote. "Tourists in livery teams on their way from the Snake Dance of the Grand Cañon, 'doing Zuni'; Mexicans bound for Atarki; teamsters on their way to Black Rock or Kelsey's store, or Mor-mons on one of their never ceasing journeys, with Indians, Navajo and Zuñi, picturesque and apparently devoid of care." Zuni had never been as isolated as Frank Cushing had made it seem in *My Adventures in Zuñi*, and in 1902 Culin had already noted how little affected by the traffic the pueblo seemed, de-spite "the location of the pueblo on a well traveled road, with numerous visitors, both traders and sightseer[s]." Now it positively bustled, and tourists had made it a regular stop.[35]

Culin himself took more time to see the sights on this trip than he had before. He made a few purchases from traders and others who had acquired old things, but the bulk of his acquisitions came in lump form from Andrew Vanderwagen, who had again amassed a collection of dolls and masks for him. Culin hired a Zuni man, evidently one who had produced items for the 1903 collection Vanderwagen had assembled, to make some turquoise jewelry for him. But for the most part he observed dances, explored the countryside, and collected information from Nick Graham and other informants. His expedition report, like that for 1902, was largely filled with observations of a Zuni dance, this time a corn dance that Culin reported had not been performed for some years, and with descriptions of life in the pueblo.*[36]

In his expedition reports, Culin reflected little on the ends and ethics of his collecting. In one of his stories, however, he considered quite directly the ethical problems of collecting among tribes like the Zuni. "The Treasure Cave of the Little Fire" seems to be based on efforts he made during his 1904 stay in the pueblo to find out what he could about some ancient shrines that Vanderwagen had plundered for his 1903 collection.

My first problem when I examined the material I bought from the Missionary was to find what it was and where it came from. The masks were easy. He had tagged them all. But there were

---

*Inquiries to Nick Graham about the corn dance unearthed the fact that the dance included burlesques, and that several years ago the Newe:kwe (a sort of Zuni clown) had burlesqued Matilda Stevenson: "She arrived in an old, broken-down wagon laden with empty cans and bottles, and a forlorn camp outfit. She was accompanied by a young Negro girl, her cook, and a company of soldiers with Capitan and other officers. They camped in the plaza, built a fire, and cooked supper, Mrs. Stevenson never ceasing to curse the cook."

six old wooden images that looked as if they had been carved in Assyria or Babylonia. Without doubt they were the war gods from the cave on the mountain. There were ancient painted pottery jars; for a surity [sic] the jars from the Siatasha shrine. But there were also an enormous number of painted wooden tablets, of prayer wands and sacrificial offerings whose age was attested by color as delicate and entrancing as the lustres of Rakka and Sultanabad. They seemed to have come all from the same place, but where?[37]

Culin's alter ego in this story is troubled by the ethics of his acquisition. He at least partially pardons the missionary who assembled the collection by suggesting that it was the result of a well-intentioned, if perhaps misguided, devotion to his own religion: "It was evident that the Missionary in his crusade against idolatry had cleaned up all the sacred places in the vicinity of the pueblo." But the narrator has no such excuse: "I am conscious always of my superior virtue, but I had not only acquired this stolen property, but been privy to its theft as well." He reconciles himself quickly, though, announcing the matter closed in the very next sentence: "The sacred objects could not be replaced. They had cost a large sum of money. I must make the best of them."

Making the best of this collection requires that two obligations be fulfilled. First, the narrator has to find out what he can about the artifacts, especially where they come from. Returning to the pueblo the following year, he carries detailed color drawings of the items with him, eager to learn what people can tell him about them. And he begins to sense the second obligation: to reunite the war gods he has acquired with others that earlier treasure seekers have removed from the shrine. This he considers a respectable alternative to repatriation, which he deems impossible, though he is vague on exactly why. "If I could not return them to their cave, I could at least reassemble them in the

respectable shelter of a plate glass case where they would be protected from neglect and decay."

Finding the rest of the war-god figures is not an easy job.
Culin's hero has no idea who took them (though he refers to
them as "vandals") or what has become of them. He thinks back
over the adventures of his friend Cushing, discovering the treasure cave but losing its treasures,* then, in a few short lines,
sums up the difference between his work and his friend's: he
has his narrator admit that he "had no practice in the art of clairvoyance" and so must resort, like Culin, to the more mundane
methods of the world of the market. He advertises: "Lost, Six
ancient carved war gods. Liberal Reward, No questions asked."

In fact, this advertisement circulates by word of mouth, not in
the press, but, as Culin noted elsewhere, the region's informal
networks of gossip and news were extremely effective. "Almost
before nightfall," the narrator has the information he wants.
Three of the images are in the possession of a former trader who
has moved away and set up a shop; another is being used by a
clergyman in California to illustrate lectures; and news of the
others comes to light. The narrator reports his own bit of magic.
He manages to take possession of all but one of the twelve gods
he had sought: "I need go no further than to say with due mod-
esty that all but one of the twelve gods are now protected safely
by a plate glass case."

What about the first task, finding out about the other artifacts,
especially a set of painted tablets and wands? He takes long
walks with someone he calls the Wizard (possibly Nick Graham,
whom the Zunis at one point accused of witchcraft). The Wizard
teaches his secrets of Zuni ceremonial practices, relates tales of
Hopi magic, and acts as guide as the narrator shows his drawings
around, but they can find no one in the pueblo who is willing to

*See Chapter 3, page 99.

recognize the items. Even the missionary refuses to talk, though "once when business was dull and mission funds low he disappeared over night and returned the next morning with a burlap bag filled with more painted tablets and colored wands which without delay I put carefully out of sight."

Apparently the narrator has overcome his qualms about receiving stolen merchandise, or perhaps his efforts to preserve the war gods have given him a sense of redemption, though he seems also to have come to believe that the Indians didn't really begrudge him his collections. Not only have they forgiven him his role in "the affair of the Missionary's masks" (perhaps a reference to "Blue Beard's Chamber") but, he suggests, they actually have a new rapport with him: they seem, Culin writes, "to recognize a certain humanizing influence in dishonesty which has not escaped the attention of our own philosophers."

The narrator occupies himself by observing the annual celebrations of the Little Fire Society and, afterward, by looking for someone from the society who will sell him the altar they made for the ceremony; he is also interested in finding an authentic house to have as a setting for the altar. (The one where the ceremony was actually held, though authentic enough for the Zunis, is too modern for his taste.)

In the end, the narrator learns what he wants to know not through careful research, "diplomacy and bribery, the pressure of necessity and the blandishments of friendship," but quite by accident:

> A little Indian boy who spent his days with bow and arrow watching sheep with whom I sometimes walked when the Wizard was tending his shop took me once into a side canon where high up in a rocky projection was the black mouth of a cave. Steep as was the face of the rock there were marks of a recent trail and at its foot a single old painted plume stick. I would have recognized it among ten thousand. The mystery was clear.

I looked at the boy. In a whisper he uttered, "the ancient shrine of the Little Fire." It was none other than Teantsali's [sic] treasure cave.

With this Culin symbolically completed two separate quests. His narrator locates the source of the treasures in his own collection, and he has concluded an adventure of Cushing's, finding by chance what Cushing had found by clairvoyance and lost to the vigilance of his Zuni hosts. "It had been a long pursuit," the narrator concludes, "but now when it was over I would have had it no other way and when we returned to the pueblo I gave a bright silver dollar to the wondering boy." The fictionalized adventure ends as flatly as did Culin's 1904 night ride with the church columns. He doesn't have his narrator ask the boy to peek inside the cave, let alone wander about in it himself. He tells us nothing about the history or spiritual meaning of the sacred place. For the narrator, as for Culin, the object of the quest is carefully circumscribed: what matters is possession, in its most concrete form, and provenance.

The beginning and end of this story seem oddly incongruous, yet they reveal something important about Culin. He started out by acquiring a remarkable collection of rare sacred artifacts that, because they were stolen, presented an ethical dilemma. It was not a unique dilemma, however. Every anthropologist who collected sacred objects wrestled with it, and in the end most of them found ways to justify keeping the objects, usually talking of the inevitable "natural" disappearance of peoples and their material cultures, and of the redemptive, preservationist function of their work. Culin, too, used these arguments to assuage his guilt, particularly the preservationist one, but his experience, at least as this story presents it, was one not of soul-searching but of transactions.

His immediate assertion that "the sacred objects could not be replaced" makes no sense on the surface. Vanderwagen certainly knew the location of the shrine, and Culin himself found it. If neither of them could put the objects back, certainly they could be given to the Zunis, who would have figured out what to do with them. What Culin seemed to be acknowledging was that the very removal of the objects from the shrine deprived them of use and meaning (or even angered the gods to whom they had been offered). Alienated, they had entered the market and could not thereafter reclaim their sacred status; they were now and forever commodities. And "they had cost a large sum of money." This argument is neither sophisticated nor intrinsically logical, but it seems to have allayed Culin's moral qualms. Having reunited the alienated war gods and found the cave from which the objects had been removed, his narrator redeems his sin of complicity in the theft by means of simple, concrete acts of acquisition and research.

For Culin, collecting was a professional endeavor, and his success in securing often very rare artifacts made him famous. The scope of his collection from Zuni, the work he did in verifying what he had and where it came from, and, most of all, the care with which he arranged his purchases in museum exhibits when he returned to Brooklyn all qualified him to take his place beside Cushing and Stevenson as an expert on Zuni. Yet his methods were very different. Though he made extended visits to the pueblo and worked, with interpreters, to unearth information about social practices related to the artifacts he collected, in many ways he was more a tourist than an anthropological fieldworker.[38]

Culin was never engaged in the social life of the pueblo as Cushing and Stevenson were. Cushing believed that he needed to step as much as possible inside the skin of a Zuni to learn to see and feel the world as a Zuni might. Stevenson wanted to be a presence at Zuni, to see Zuni customs for herself, and to reconstruct Zuni cultural practices from her firsthand work with informants who knew all the words and all the stories. In both cases, they based their work on their physical presence at the center of Zuni. Culin remained more removed. His expedition reports and other writings reveal relatively little engagement with the Zunis. Not only did he buy a significant portion of his collection from a white trader but often when he wanted information about his purchases he consulted traders, missionaries, and other ethnologists rather than Zunis. When he did buy things in the pueblo, he relied heavily on the mediation of his interpreters, and showed little interest in exploring the shrines and caves that other collectors, including Vanderwagen, found to be such rich sources for old and even ancient artifacts. He was willing to get involved himself where necessary, as in securing the church columns, but he was more than happy to let other people do the procuring for him. In fact, his experiences at Zuni, particularly those he wrote about fictionally, were more vicarious than real, the dangers he faced almost always more fantasy than fact.

Culin had more in common with the competitive collectors and tourists he encountered in increasing numbers at Zuni over the years than he did with ethnologists. He came to see and to buy, not to engage and experience. Cushing and Stevenson had first come to Zuni before the rail links across the continent were complete, astride mules they had ridden for days across the desert. But by the time Culin first visited the Southwest in 1900, the railroad was complete, and comfortable railroad hotels were being built (with, not incidentally, lively centers for the sale of Indian artifacts). And Culin made his first trip in the company of George Dorsey, the ethnologist from the Field Museum, who had learned to use the railroad effectively in order to give him an edge in what he perceived as the race to salvage Native American artifacts from the region. Culin's milieu was urban America, and when he worked to preserve Zuni's material heritage, as

Cushing and Stevenson had worked to preserve its cultural heritage, it was for urban Americans, for visitors in Brooklyn, not for any friends he might have made in the pueblo.[39]

Culin mounted two Zuni exhibits at the Brooklyn Museum: the first, the centerpiece of the new ethnological hall, in 1905; the second, an impressive effort at reinstallation, when the museum expanded in 1925. The exhibit was his forte, artifacts a medium that he manipulated with genius. He was adept at getting things on display fast, almost as soon as he returned from the field. This was in striking contrast to ethnologists like Franz Boas, who liked to withhold objects from public view until they had been carefully studied and labeled. Like a department-store magnate, Culin got his goods out on the floor before the competition did. And his exhibits had continuity and comprehensiveness. In other museums, collections had various origins and creative sources: different ethnologists and collectors made bits and pieces available in the course of their work. At the Brooklyn Museum, Culin did virtually all the collecting, the commissioning of replicas, and the design of the exhibits. When he mounted an exhibit, it was, in its own right, an individually authored work, as much as any published piece by Cushing or Stevenson.[40]

Culin completed the Southwest hall in 1907 and added other Native American exhibits until, in 1912, with an exhibit about the Northwest coast, he finished his work on Native Americans. In fact, he had given up collecting Native American artifacts three years earlier, and feeling, like other American anthropologists, that the Native American field had been exhausted, turned his attention to Europe and, once again, to Asia. In the years between 1912 and the opening of a dramatically new ethnology hall in 1925, he moved further and further away from mainstream anthropology, focusing instead on aesthetics and on the commercial use he thought might be made of the artistic principles of pre-industrial peoples.[41]

His attention returned to Zuni when the Brooklyn Museum gave the Department of Ethnology expanded space in a new wing. He started to plan a reinstallation in 1925, nearly twenty years after his last ethnological trip to the pueblo. The new hall he envisioned was substantially more ambitious than the one he had opened in 1905, including not only his Native American collections but Oceanic, African, and Asian material as well. The Rainbow House exhibit, which he named after a Zuni shrine, brought Culin's long professional life into one big room, and served as a sort of architectural memoir for him. (He was sixty-seven years old.) He was now more interested in the aesthetics of his collections, concerned more with things of the spirit. The romantic spiritualism that marked his fiction, too, became more pronounced, and in the Rainbow House he gave it full rein. He felt free, even compelled, to insist on his own interpretation of the things he had gathered together.[42]

In installing the objects, he showed his fascination with color and the lessons he had learned in studying not only department-store windows but the youthful exuberance of pre-industrial patterns; he assigned a different, vibrant color to each of the cultures represented. The pink of the sunrise was the color for Zuni, which provided a frame for the entire exhibit. California's native people were represented by deep red, while "a blue of the depths mark[ed] the islands of the Caribbean Sea and a tawny yellow the great South American continent; the green of shallow waters the islands of the Pacific, and the deep green of the tropical jungle shot with sunlight, the great river valley of the African Congo." His vision of these cultures (the Asian portions of the exhibit were not yet installed when he opened the hall) was nostalgic, the gaze of a man of advanced years fondly looking back not only over his own life but over a continuum of cultures.[43]

"I believe one should be free to choose," he told a group of New York City art teachers at the opening of the hall in December 1925, "whether the past be seen as a kind of inferno, diversified by murder and punctuated by crime, or as a joyous period of creative effort as I realize it from things of the past which I have made my friends and enticed into telling me their tales." There is a strange darkness in the vision of the past that he rejected, perhaps a reference to his own collecting crimes, perhaps something less personal. But Culin chose the brighter view, and Rainbow House was his optimistic tribute to youth. He equated pre-industrial peoples with children, steadfastly maintaining the evolutionary view of cultures even though, by 1925, this was being displaced by Franz Boas's cultural relativism and by the ascent of university-trained anthropologists who shared Boas's views. He suggested quite openly that cultures like Zuni and the others he grouped it with, though chronologically older than his own, in fact represented the childhood of man, an innocence and exuberance lost to his own, more sophisticated people. "I used to be known among the Zuñi from my persistent inquiries as Inotai, 'Old Thing'," he told the teachers, "and I was in fact old beside the oldest member of the tribe, but I learned something of the secret of youth and its happiness from them, not to speak of the story of the Rainbow House, from which I borrowed the idea as well as the name of the new gallery of our museum." He exhorted them to nourish their pupils' connection to nature, that element of freshness that, as children, they shared with pre-industrial people; and he suggested that through children and through cultures like Zuni, one might capture some of the child-like wonder and happiness that were lost to more mature cultures and people.[44]

The Rainbow House exhibit was a last, beautiful tribute to an ethnological vision that had already been eclipsed. In it Culin incorporated the latest ideas in museum display, moving decisively away from the dull tones of earlier archival exhibits and bringing the voice of the curator firmly to the fore, even though he still claimed that he was only "trying to coax and arrange [things] to tell [their] story to the world." Fearing the loss of something spiritually important, Culin fashioned a temple in Brooklyn in which it might be preserved:

The place where I myself am now standing is the Center of the World. I say this in no spirit of paradox. This Gallery of Ethnology of the Brooklyn Museum, which you today are assembled to open and dedicate, is not merely a symbol of the people of the world. It is intended as the home of their spirit. The science of ethnology has to do with the spirit, with the consciousness of peoples, and this gallery is intended as a place for its concrete expression.[45]

CONCLUSION:
ZUNI LEGACY

———

Frank Cushing did most of his work on Zuni during his first long stay in the pueblo from 1879 to 1884. After he thwarted the attempts of a senator's son-in-law to usurp a piece of land that contained a crucial Zuni spring, he was pressured to relinquish his job there as a representative of the Bureau of American Ethnology. But he returned to the Southwest and to the pueblo in 1886 as the director of the Hemenway South-West Archaeological Expedition, an ambitious project financed by a wealthy Bostonian, Mary Hemenway, with whom he had become acquainted. He continued to direct the project until 1889, when ill health forced him to return east, though he was bedeviled by a jealous reluctance to delegate authority to other members of the expedition team, by a frustrating inability to produce written reports (a problem that had also marked his work with the Bureau of American Ethnology), and by a creative imagination that threatened to cross the boundaries of scientific proof.

After leaving the Hemenway Expedition, Cushing returned to the bureau, spending the years 1892–1894 working on exhibits and presentations for the Chicago World's Fair and writing up his work on Zuni. It was during this period that he wrote his "Outlines of Zuni Creation Myths," weaving Zuni myths into his own master narrative. In the last years of his life, he turned his attention to archaeological discoveries in Florida. Again he stirred up controversy over the efficiency and authenticity of his work. Cushing died accidentally in 1900, after a lifetime of ill health, by choking on a bone at a dinner in Washington. He left behind a legacy that mixed moments of great brilliance with a record of administrative failures and sometimes questionable judgment.[1]

Matilda Stevenson continued her work in ethnology of the Southwest until her death in 1915. Her last published work on the pueblo, a study of its ethnobotany, was included in the Bureau of American Ethnology's annual report for 1908–1909 (published in 1915). Like Cushing, she found herself increasingly out of step with other anthropologists as she grew older, the object of both personal ridicule and professional criticism, including Stewart Culin's report of the Zunis' burlesque of her efforts, though within the carnivalesque spirit of the Zuni dance her sense of belonging at Zuni was probably confirmed by the performance. Younger anthropologists considered her imperious and foolish and questioned both the seriousness of her work and the affection she claimed her southwestern Native acquaintances felt for her. Her reception in the Bureau of American Ethnology's Washington offices had never been entirely cordial, and she now spent more and more of each year on her ranch in New Mexico, finally finding the messy, mixed culture of frontier life there more congenial than the capital. Like Cushing, she found it hard to complete reports of her work, and some accounts picture her as a rather bitter old woman, given to drinking too much, and increasingly occupied with an exasperating civil litigation rather than with professional accomplishments. Her book, however, continued to be a vital source for anyone interested in Zuni anthropology. Some years after her death, Margaret Lewis, a Zuni by marriage and a rich source of information for the anthropologist Elsie Clews Parsons, asked Parsons for a copy of Stevenson's book to help with a book that she herself was hoping to write. Alfred Kroeber, who, like Parsons, began his work at Zuni in the 1910s and 1920s, found Stevenson's work more useful than Cushing's, because it was more comprehensive and less imaginative.[2]

At the Brooklyn Museum, Stewart Culin moved easily away from ethnology toward the study of aesthetics, apparently little concerned with the judgments of professional anthropologists, with whom he had only tangentially associated himself in any case. His last collecting trip to Zuni was in 1907, and by 1912 he had finished his Native American collections. He seems to have been comfortable with his life and work in his later years in a way that Cushing and Stevenson were not. He died in 1929.

In 1909, just a generation after Cushing and Stevenson first reached Zuni, anthropologists and archaeologists connected with the American Museum of Natural History in New York began work on an ambitious project aimed at a "general outline of culture history for the Southwest." Initially focused on the pueblos of the Rio Grande Valley, east of Zuni, the Archer M. Huntington survey encompassed both living and ancient cultures and represented a new attempt at systematic, comprehensive, regional investigation. In 1915, it was broadened to include Zuni as well as the area's nomadic peoples (the Navajos and the Apaches), the Hopi pueblos in Colorado, and some Anasazi villages.[3] The team that arrived at Zuni that summer included Alfred Kroeber and Leslie Spier. Also working on this regional portrait were Nils C. Nelson, Earl H. Morris, Pliny Earle Goddard, Robert H. Lowie, and A. V. Kidder.

Elsie Clews Parsons, still an amateur but eager to establish both her own professional credentials and a connection with scientists from the American Museum and from Columbia University (the two were closely related), paid her first visit to Zuni that summer as well, missing Kroeber by a few days but successfully staking out a claim to anthropological exploration in the pueblos. During the next few years, she returned on her own and with Kroeber, and in 1919 she persuaded Franz Boas, the guiding genius of the new cultural anthropology emanating from Columbia, to visit the Southwest as well. By 1924 Ruth Benedict, under the guidance of Boas and the watchful eye of Parsons, had begun the work that would culminate in 1934 with *Patterns of Culture*. She and Ruth Bunzel, another protégé of Boas and Parsons, pursued their fieldwork side by side in the pueblo over the years. "The Ruths," as Parsons dubbed them, worked together nicely despite Parsons's skepticism that two women would do anything other than "waste each other's time."[4]

Thus before the new century was a decade old, a new style of anthropology based on radically different theoretical underpinnings had begun to move toward Zuni. These new anthropologists stressed a uniformity of approach and an appreciation for the connections among, rather than the isolated development of, cultures that shared geographic regions. The deployment of many distinguished scientists all at once, with coordinated marching orders, would have appealed to John Wesley Powell. But, despite the universalizing tendencies of evolutionary anthropological theory, the anthropologists who came of age during his tenure at the Bureau of American Ethnology were primarily interested in the differences among people. They worked alone for the most part (or felt they did, though they relied heavily on Native American assistants), and they could see individual cultures as discrete entities in a way that was probably easier in the nineteenth century than in the twentieth. Parsons described their approach sardonically as "Walpi, the world," separating each culture from those around it and treating each as a self-contained world, sufficient unto itself. Though the description is not entirely fair to either Cushing or Stevenson, she was troubled by what she saw as their failure to integrate information on related cultures into their studies of Zuni.[5]

As the locus of anthropological study moved away from Washington geographically and from the museum to the university institutionally, the historical particularism that Franz Boas had begun to articulate as early as 1887 in the pages of *Science* magazine gradually gained importance. Historical relativism was in part an unexpected consequence of the first awkward attempts at systematic collecting by the generation of anthropologists who invented fieldwork. Despite their devotion to the ideas of evolutionary anthropology, they found that the more specific the data they collected, the less likely it seemed that universal patterns of mind and fixed phases of cultural development explained the facts they had discovered. The new practice of fieldwork, however tainted by its connection to an evolutionary theory that was later discredited, encouraged anthropologists to study the history as well as the culture of indigenous societies, and the more they learned of the particular circumstances of the individual societies they studied, the less likely they were to subscribe to broad, universal theories of human development. The grand organizing schemes of the nineteenth century gave way to an appreciation of the fragmentary, relativistic nature of experience and the inescapable interconnectedness of human societies.[6]

Frank Cushing, Matilda Stevenson, and to a lesser extent Stewart Culin had helped lay the groundwork for this new historical particularism, though the paradigm that had shaped their own researches in the field led to an evolutionary dead end. Like dinosaurs, who now survive only in the evolutionary history of birds, these salvage ethnologists were a vital bridge between the amateur, ahistorical, and progressive anthropology of the nineteenth century and the professional, historical, and relativistic anthropology of the twentieth. In fact, they themselves did little speculating on the evolutionary meta-narrative their research supported. It was people like John Wesley Powell, who relied on their work, who concerned themselves with grand schemes. The raw materials they supplied supported very different narratives in later hands.

In many ways they conceived of their work in the same way that Clark Wissler, the curator of anthropology at the American Museum of Natural History, described that of the 1909 Huntington expedition; Wissler was sympathetic to the ideas of both generations and mediated between the two. But Cushing, Stevenson, Culin, and their generation combined ideas about scientific method and systematic study with the special influence of "salvage," which pushed them toward collecting and preserving and away from the work of interpretation. The salvage moment over, for better or worse, the next generation had to concern itself with the interrelatedness of societies, when, in Elsie Clews Parsons's words, "two civilizations get tangled up and fuse their patterns perceptibly." The later anthropologists were just as avid about collecting, just as taken with exploring forbidden shrines and acquiring sacred artifacts, but they could no longer ignore the historical forces that had shaped the world they were studying.[7]

The focus of anthropological work became both broader and narrower. Zuni was studied in its regional context, and in its relations with other cultures that might reveal its migratory history and shed light on when the Zuni region was settled and at what pace. Among Parsons's contributions, for example, was a study linking Taos, the northernmost of the Rio Grande pueblos, with traditions from the Plains. She and others concentrated on the diffusion, melding, and mutating of cultural knowledge and on the particular historical circumstances that produced things that may have looked alike but in fact had different meanings. Their understanding of the processes of cultural development allowed for complexities that evolutionary anthropologists had not easily acknowledged.

Salvage ethnologists, who clung to the belief that they studied pure cultures and rescued the artifactual record from the inevitable pollution of contact with the industrial world, often pushed aside evidence of the mixing of cultures. The photographer Edward Curtis excised evidence of white encroachment from his stunning record of Native American faces, literally narrowing his focus to leave out telegraph lines and train tracks. When Matilda Stevenson saw that a photograph she had taken of an altar from a pueblo near Zuni included two ceramic dogs from China, she quietly had them cropped out of the reproduction that she included in her published study. The anthropologists who followed her embraced rather than ignored these strange juxtapositions, looking not for some pure past but for clues to the adaptive capacities of people and cultures. Assuming that cultures like Zuni were adapting rather than declining or dying out, anthropologists from the Boas school focused on continuity and change rather than on disjuncture.[8]

The picture of Zuni that Frank Cushing, Matilda Stevenson, and Stewart Culin created was in many ways like Stevenson's altar. In it, Zuni was frozen in time, caught in a moment before contact with the culture of the United States changed it forever. This stylized representation of Zuni circulated widely among white Americans at the turn of the century. In their writings and lectures, their exhibits, and, perhaps most of all, through their exposition work, these three individuals literally moved their Zuni, in the form of thousands of artifacts and reams of paper, out of the Southwest and into the halls of their museums and the pages of their books. Like some parallel world encountered by the starship *Enterprise*, their Zuni spun off, unhinged in space but stuck in time, to exist parallel to the Zuni that went on living in New Mexico.

The image that remained when they were finished with their work on Zuni highlighted the contrasts it offered with their own society. The potency of that image is perhaps best measured in Ruth Benedict's *Patterns of Culture*, the most widely read anthropological work to come out of the pueblo. Benedict, a passionate advocate of cultural relativism, argued that Zuni was a consensus-oriented, anti-individualistic, harmony-loving alternative in a world still reeling from its first total war and flirting dangerously with militarism and totalitarianism; Zuni was an "Apollonian" oasis in a "Dionysian" world. Though she took great pains to make a place for exceptions, she was struck by the integration and cohesiveness of Zuni culture, even after a fifty-year assault by the forces of the market and United States culture.

Benedict saw herself as a crusader against the excesses of evolutionary anthropology. And yet the Zuni she writes about in *Patterns of Culture* preserves many of the assumptions that Cushing, Stevenson, and Culin had in their representations of the pueblo: that Zuni was molded out of the land itself, that it maintained a unity with nature—the romantic nature both celebrated and mourned in the cultivated city parks of Frederick Law Olmstead's generation, which preceded theirs. Zuni's ethnic homogeneity, reinforced by an intricate system of overlapping clans and societies, ensured, even required, a level of consensus that verged on compulsion. The Zunis walked together in a social dance as carefully choreographed as their ceremonial rituals. The magnificent costumed dancers who from time to time appeared in their courtyards signaled not only a colored, patterned vibrancy that was lost to the black-and-white off-the-racks crowds on urban streets but a religion that was inseparable from everyday life, an intimate connection with the gods. Zuni was a lost moment in the American past, a classless nation of farmers who served their gods and their society without suffering the segmentation and alienation of the American present.[9]

Frank Cushing, Matilda Stevenson, and Stewart Culin succeeded in capturing that lost moment. Ironically, Zuni itself survived them, and it continues to attract anthropologists who study their works for many reasons (there is even a study of the effect of anthropologists on Zuni).[10] But Zuni was not the preface to an American historical narrative, as the generation of evolutionary anthropologists had hoped. Anthropology changed and Zuni changed, and in the end both were subjected to a more rigorous, if more specialized and isolated, discipline.

It is partly because the Zunis (and a surprising number of other Native American tribes) continued to exist, if not exactly to thrive, that evolutionary anthropologists could never deliver on the grand historical narrative their early theoretical work promised. For they presumed that there would soon be no more Indians, that after the forces of attrition and assimilation had done their work only an ideal primitive ancestor would remain, an image that could conveniently transcend race. For white Americans, including most anthropologists, could only abstractly and universally conceive of themselves as descendants of such dark-skinned neighbors. They abhorred the idea of mixing the white race with others, not only sexually but spatially. They did not want to interbreed with Native Americans, and they did not want to share the land with them.

A conflict between the anthropologists' scientific theories and practical political policy was also responsible for their failure. Their theory posited the capacity of all people and all cultures to evolve to the top of the pyramid of civilization, and assumed that these native cultures would not do so because there was no time. They were doomed because they were too late. The juggernaut of industrial society was expanding too fast and would not wait for them to catch up. The best the anthropologists could argue for was that Native Americans could assimilate. Their cultures were doomed, but they themselves might survive in the "civilized" white world—if they stopped being Indians.[11]

This fatalistic conclusion was proudly imperialistic. Though anthropologists and their audiences at fairs and in museums gloried in the uniqueness of native artifacts, they had no model for the coexistence of diverse cultures, only a nuanced rationale for a teleological history in which the most advanced cultures dominated. In his presidential address to the International Congress of Anthropology at the 1893 World's Fair in Chicago, Daniel Brinton, Stewart Culin's friend and mentor in Philadelphia, outlined the process by which more highly civilized nations absorbed others, a process that, he argued, could be deduced from the bloodlines of a nation's people as clearly as from its history. For Brinton, anthropology revealed the inevitable victory of modern nations, nations that were monotheistic, democratic, and possessed of a sense of humanity sufficiently broad to incorporate more provincial models within it. The pre-civilized past, though instructive, was not, for Brinton, anything to be particularly proud of, or anything worth preserving, except in the halls of museums, which were, in Barbara Kirshenblatt-Gimblett's perceptive words, "tomb[s] with a view."[12]

United States policy toward the nations within its borders also thwarted any historical narrative that linked Native Americans to white Americans, however abstractly. Anthropologists may have been convinced of the imminent demise of native cultures, may have cherished and tried to protect the subjects of their studies, but others, interested in immediate economic issues, pressed hard for the right to treat Native Americans like anyone else, in particular to buy and sell their land, and to be protected from any organized native resistance to their plans. Proponents of policies like the Dawes Severalty Act of 1887, which carved communally held native lands into plots allotted to individuals and sold off the remainder, freely used the language of evolutionary anthropology to argue that welcoming Native Americans into the world of private property and free enterprise would speed up their evolution and acknowledge their equality. Though some anthropologists, most notably Alice Fletcher, who worked among the Omahas, supported such policies with the best of intentions, many others, including John Wesley Powell, found themselves at odds with policymakers in search of a way around evolutionary time. They were used to dealing with Native Americans relatively abstractly, as harmless remnants of a bygone time. But for many Westerners, and for Americans in any state who had Native Americans as neighbors, Native Americans were not at all abstract and not particularly harmless. The tension between these two attitudes reinforced the separation from Native Americans that had been established when their artifacts were put behind glass walls and in wooden cases.[13]

Finally, the possibility of a synthesized narrative of the American past was undermined by the tourist industry's appropriation of certain stylized aspects of anthropological work. Tourism came to the Southwest only a few years after anthropology did, when the rail link between Chicago and Los Angeles was completed in 1880. In 1882, in partnership with the Atchison, Topeka and Santa Fe Railway, the Fred Harvey Company, famous for establishing the first civilized railroad restaurants and dining cars, built a luxury hotel at the Las Vegas Hot Springs in New Mexico. In 1901, after a decade of experiments with stagecoaches, the railway began service on a spur line from Williams, Arizona, to the Grand Canyon for cross-country passengers who wished to make an "Indian Detour" under the Harvey aegis; a year later, Harvey opened up an Indian building adjacent to its palatial Alvarado Hotel, both just steps away from the railroad tracks in Albuquerque. In 1903, the railway published *Indians of the Southwest*, a guide to the cultures of the region specially designed for train passengers and written by Stewart Culin's onetime traveling companion George Dorsey, of the Field Museum. The text told passengers how to explore the region, but it was also intended for those who were content to do their adventuring from the train. In 1905, Harvey, again in concert with the Atchison, Topeka and Santa Fe, built the rustic and luxurious El Tovar Hotel at the rim of the Grand Canyon. One attraction there was Hopi House, a replica of a pueblo designed by the architect Mary Colter and lived in by Hopis who made and sold their crafts during the day, sang and danced for hotel guests in the evening, and slept in Hopi House, authentically, at night. The Harvey Company also had a lucrative side business selling artifacts to museums, private collectors, and tourists; meanwhile, it enabled visitors to stroll across the grounds into a simulated anthropological experience.[14]

Anthropology had often been closely connected with tourism. Certainly the Midway at the Chicago World's Fair, which was overseen by the Ethnology Department, headed by Frederick W. Putnam of the Harvard Peabody Museum, offered simulated ethnological experiences, as did more sober exhibits in the Anthropology Building. But in the Southwest anthropological tourism drove development. Where other regions of the United States were developed after the Civil War by settlers and industrial entrepreneurs, this area was popularly viewed as a wasteland. It was the peculiar genius of men at the Atchison, Topeka and Santa Fe and at Fred Harvey to see its potential as a sort of precursor to the modern theme park. They set out to lure tourists to the region, and the attraction they offered was Indians. The Albuquerque Indian Building contained Native American treasures from across the continent. In a masterful piece of marketing, Harvey stopped the trains on the tracks just outside, drew passengers across a court where Native Americans sold their crafts, and then enticed them into the museum, where signs advised them that these items were not for sale; elsewhere, customers could watch native people at work. Then, finally, they reached the salesroom, where, their appetites whetted by what they could not have, they might purchase souvenirs. So even passengers who did not want to break their trip and stay at the hotel or tour the countryside were encouraged to have a brief encounter with the still-exotic cultures assembled in the Harvey marketplace.[15]

This tourist version of anthropology arose with the profession itself, and the two intersected, not only because the experience orchestrated by the Harvey Company and those created by anthropologists for world's fairs (most of which included live Indians) were similar but because they shared the work of acquisition. Many collectors of Native American artifacts at this time, whether they were private individuals like George Heye and William Randolph Hearst or public institutions like the American Museum of Natural History, bought artifacts from the Harvey Company's Indian Department.

The crossover between tourism and science attracted funding for serious expeditions and collections, but it also distracted anthropologists from pure study and hastened the very degradation of native cultures that had made salvage ethnology so urgent. In the end, its excesses were one reason that professional anthropologists left the museums. In anthropology as conceived by Franz Boas and his followers, objects moved from the center to the periphery; they were still important, but as corroboration rather than culmination.

The old evolutionary narrative gave way to the pressures of politics and everyday realities, and changed with anthropology's new focus. Indian societies remained a popular subject, and Zuni continued to attract the attention of both serious students and popular audiences. The Huntington Survey, staffed by a remarkable number of young anthropologists who later became prominent, helped to lay the groundwork for Ruth Benedict's *Patterns of Culture*, as had Matilda Stevenson, Frank Cushing, and Stewart Culin.

Patterns of Culture briefly sketched three relatively primitive cultures: the Zunis of New Mexico; a society of islanders known as the Dobuans, who lived off the coast of New Guinea; and the Kwakiutl, a tribe from the northwest coast of North America among whom Boas had done much of his original anthropological research. But more important than Benedict's analysis of any one of these peoples was her brilliant, accessible articulation of the idea that there existed not a single pattern of culture, as followers of Lewis Henry Morgan had argued, but a multiplicity of patterns. The idea of a multiplicity of patterns of culture released human society from the determinism of the evolutionary narrative and shattered its assumption of superiority. In Benedict's new anthropology, human beings were the agents of their own cultures, fashioning creative responses to the basic problems of perpetuating their own lives and the lives of their societies. The idea of a divine pattern yielded to an appreciation for human ones.

Within this treatise on the relativity of cultures, and on the element of human choice in the development of social values and practices, Benedict placed her portrait of Zuni. Like her portraits of the Dobuans and the Kwakiutls, it stresses the coherence of the society. Benedict believed that every social practice emanated from a core of cultural values, and she was particularly interested in what she saw as a fundamental dichotomy: that societies seemed to be oriented either toward an individualist yearning to challenge the world or toward a socially grounded yearning to live within its bounds. Borrowing from Friedrich Nietzsche, who in turn had borrowed from Greek tragedy, she labeled these methods of arriving at the "values of existence" Dionysian and Apollonian. Dionysian societies arrived at their values through, in Nietzsche's words, "the annihilation of the ordinary bounds and limits of existence." An individual rooted in a Dionysian culture, Benedict went on, "seeks to attain in his most valued moments escape from the boundaries imposed upon him by his five senses, to break through into another order of experience. The desire of the Dionysian, in personal experience or in ritual, is to press through it toward a certain psychological state, to achieve excess." Apollonian peoples, like those of the New Mexican pueblos, including Zuni, were, in contrast, suspicious of this devotion to excess:

> The Apollonian distrusts all this, and has often little idea of the nature of such experiences. He finds means to outlaw them from his conscious life. He "knows but one law, measure in the Hellenic sense." He keeps the middle of the road, stays within the known map, does not meddle with disruptive psychological states. In Nietzsche's fine phrase, even in the exaltation of the dance he "remains what he is, and retains his civic name."[16]

Benedict's portrait of Zuni is framed by this conception of the Apollonian orientation. Everything about the society she describes is marked by restraint and by a concern for the whole that outweighs the claims of individuals. The dramatic ritual dances, which struck observers like Stewart Culin as vaguely orgiastic, were, to Benedict, carefully orchestrated, controlled performances whose purpose was to maintain social order. Even the violence of Zuni rituals, like the lashing Frank Cushing endured as the price of attending the Rattlesnake initiation, Benedict understood as qualitatively different from the ritual violence of other Native American societies. Where the latter aimed at intense individual experience and coveted the pain, Zuni violence, which she claimed was more ritual than real, was about exorcising demons and demonstrating social cohesion.

Zuni, for Benedict, was an essentially benevolent society. She downplayed the physical violence (most notably witchcraft cases, which, though infrequent, included torture and even murder) that was part of the pueblo's ritual life and that supported the social cohesion she admired. In contrast to Dionysian cultures, of which European culture was the most powerful exemplar for her, Zuni's emphasis on tradition, harmony, and the life of the social group seemed, despite the violence, a rational alternative. After all, Europe had recently been torn apart in a vicious, long war, and it showed no signs of having learned from the experience. That the world she described at Zuni might be claustrophobic, that it might maintain consensus at the expense of individual expression, she did not really acknowledge. Every society she studied exacted a price for its orientation, and she did not render judgments about those prices. She may have erred in painting Zuni as an alternative to individualism, as a primitive socialist utopia, but she drew no political conclusion.

It is interesting that while Benedict was writing her lyrical appreciation of Zuni, Aldous Huxley, who was also preoccupied with the frightening excesses of European progress, chose to use Zuni as the paradigmatic primitive "other" in his futuristic novel *Brave New World*. In contrast to Benedict, who avoided any explicit analysis of her own culture, the very heart of Huxley's novel was a scathing critique of the fundamental assumptions of Western society. In his book, as a foil for a future London, which has become an Apollonian utopia through cloning and drugs, Huxley invented a descendant of the Zuni pueblo, isolated on a mesa, where the social cohesion, the unity of value and purpose permeating every aspect of society, has deteriorated; the ritual and the violence remain but have no purpose. To the anesthetized visitors from London, it is precisely the individualism of experience in the pueblo that is its attraction. Sex as procreation, the connection between parents and offspring, bodies that feel— these revolt Huxley's fascinated Londoners, and the revulsion is the closest thing to real emotion they have ever felt. But Huxley's pueblo is not utopian. This pueblo world, to which Huxley gave Zuni roots, is filthy and violent, degraded by alcohol, devoid of all purpose except its function as a sort of human zoo that amuses and edifies outsiders. John Savage, raised in Zuni but descended from Londoners, is torn between two equally repellent alternatives. His final contribution to the world of his English ancestors is to reintroduce the concepts of physical pain and grotesque mortality that they have so carefully excised.

Both Benedict and Huxley thought of Zuni as a kind of alter ego for their own cultures—Benedict with guarded optimism, Huxley with something close to despair. The idea that cultures are relative, not better or worse, is found in both, and both express Benedict's central thesis that every society develops a way of life and environment that is permeated by its most cherished values. This concept of a way of life captures the modern anthropological definition of culture, which influences not only anthropologists but many historians, from those who are quite conservative to controversial practitioners of cultural studies. In the 1930s, when, according to Warren Susman, this new definition of culture first gained currency, the culture of the United States was opened up to the same sort of analysis that had heretofore been reserved for others.[17] The sense that the United States had its own way of life, its own culture, imbued with specific—not universal—values that deserved scrutiny, came in both critical and congratulatory guises. Certainly after the Second World War and during the Cold War, the congratulatory praise of the American way of life was raised to the level of a secular religion, and consumer goods became icons of the freedom and democracy denied those who lived in the Soviet orbit. But there were many who continued to cast a critical eye, among them Edmund Wilson, whose *Red, Black, Blond and Olive: Studies in Four Civilizations: Zuni, Haiti, Soviet Russia, Israel*, published in 1956, suggested an appreciation for differences and an intellectual concern for their meaning. Wilson's book, far less penetrating than either *Patterns of Culture* or *Brave New World*, was a gentle, compassionate travelogue. His Zuni owes something to Matilda Stevenson and something to Ruth Benedict, but it is not analytical; rather, it is the work of a talented essayist bringing reports back to the inhabitants of the newest world power.

In the 1960s, Robert Heinlein revived Benedict's Apollonian ideal in his novel *Stranger in a Strange Land*. This science-fiction cult classic returns, as Huxley did, to the story of *The Tempest*, the story of a child raised among aliens whose return to his own culture promises that culture redemption. In this case, a human being raised on Mars returns with a message of cooperation and harmony to an Earth that has lost its way. Shaun Reno has argued that Heinlein borrowed from Benedict in his invented Martians, though they are gentler than the Zunis; certainly the novel is a plea for consideration of a less individualistic, excessive way of life. The reference to Zuni is obscure but significant.

In the 1960s, 1970s, and 1980s, influenced by the civil-rights movement and by the American Indian Movement, anthropologists returned to Zuni. Some of them worked to peel back the layers of anthropological analysis and discover what the Zunis thought of themselves; others, with more sensitivity than their forerunners, wanted to see if they couldn't find at Zuni evidence to support new ways in which Americans might think about their own culture. (Among the latter, one of the best is Will Roscoe, whose *The Zuni Man-Woman*, which I have already mentioned, includes a careful analysis of the Zuni culture and of the concept of the berdache, which is of interest to students of gay culture.)

Dennis Tedlock, with the eye of a literary theorist as well as an anthropologist, has another focus. On trips that began in the 1960s, Tedlock listened to and recorded Zunis telling their own stories. He developed a notational system that allowed some of the cadences of Zuni speakers to accompany their stories into print. His *Finding the Center: Narrative Poetry of the Zuni Indians*, published in 1972, introduced the sort of text-centered approach to anthropology that was gaining followers in history and literature. In contrast to the records of Zuni stories kept by Matilda Stevenson and Frank Cushing, which they presented as works about the past, Tedlock's transcriptions highlight the interplay between the living narrators and the traditional tales. His is an anthropology of the living world of Zuni with all its contradictions.

Likewise, Barbara Tedlock, who accompanied her husband, Dennis, on his trips to Zuni, focused on the present rather than the past. Her 1992 book, *The Beautiful and the Dangerous: Encounters with the Zuni Indians*, recounts her efforts to find meaning in the things of Zuni today. For her, a distanced, third-person stance was not only impossible but dishonest. Heir to a decade or more of critical anthropology that called into question the "distance" of a participant-observer, Barbara Tedlock's writing self-consciously interweaves memoir and analysis. The anthropologist is part of the simultaneously familiar and strange world of the Zunis she observes. The Zunis in these books, as compelling in their own right as the Zunis described in the best of Cushing or Benedict, are people who are using the tools of their culture to deal with the daily challenges of life in the late twentieth century. Those tools include rituals that date back centuries and pickup trucks that only seem to.

What is the relationship between the Zuni presented to readers and museumgoers at the turn of the last century and the Zuni that writers continue to study at the turn of this one? There is no direct link that runs from Stevenson, Cushing, and Culin through Alfred Kroeber, Elsie Clews Parsons, and the American Museum of Natural History gang in New York in the 1910s and 1920s, from Ruth Benedict and Ruth Bunzel in the 1920s and 1930s to Huxley, Wilson, Heinlein, Roscoe, and the Tedlocks. Yet it is remarkable that so many very good minds have focused on Zuni, looking for a way to make sense of larger things.

There is still magic in that island in the desert, though it is as hard as ever to identify and unlikely ever to rescue our civilization. Even as we acknowledge that our fascination with Zuni has had at least as much to do with our own doubts and dreams as with anything they might be, or want, or need, we still live, today, with the legacy of the anthropology that went to the Southwest more than a hundred years ago. The generation of children born after the Second World War, prowling the halls of natural-history museums in the 1950s and 1960s, found there the exhibits that were part of this early anthropological story. Today, when pueblos like Zuni exist simultaneously as communities and as tourist attractions, this same generation can retrace the steps of the early collectors to the Southwest, visiting as tourists, even staying in a version of Andrew Vanderwagen's ranch. Their consciousness is tempered by the events of their youth—the movement for civil rights, the American Indian Movement, the Vietnam War—and this may intensify the emotional experience of their visits, but it also owes a good deal to an unreconstructed vision of the continent's "others" that they absorbed as children. What we make of Zuni today is complicated and perhaps a bit wistful. Sensitivity about past inequities, environmentalism, and our own forms of alienation invite us to be as myopic in our time as evolutionary anthropologists were in theirs.

One thing we should remember, however, is that Zuni is real. That it has generated so many shadows on our cave walls, so many of which are works of art in themselves, makes it difficult to remember this, and the Tedlocks suggest that this is sometimes a problem for the Zunis as well. What is it like to be simultaneously an icon and a living village? How can a society adapt and change when it exists against a version of itself that was frozen in time a century ago and that tourists still want to see when they "do" Zuni?

Despite the dire predictions of the salvage ethnologists and the wholesale removal of much of its artifactual history, Zuni still exists, balancing its cultural independence against the steady pressure of America's mass-produced homogeneity. Unlike some of its neighbors to the east—Taos and Acoma, for example—it is easy to miss if you are looking for the Zuni preserved by Cushing, Stevenson, or Culin. The terraced hill that Cushing spied glowing in the late-desert sunlight in 1879, the adobe town that seemed such a part of nature, is now, at first glance, a small southwestern town indistinguishable from hundreds of others.

The approach to Zuni from the east takes you across a broad plain, along Highway 53, which runs from Albuquerque through Zuni and into Arizona. As you get nearer, cinder-block ranch houses along the roadside become more frequent. You pass clusters of undistinguished buildings, and then, suddenly, right along the highway, which is a narrow two-lane road, there is a collection of tourist shops advertising Native American crafts, a gas station or two, a convenience store. Then, as suddenly, you are in open desert again, with scattered dwellings, a view of the distant mountains, and ahead of you is Arizona.

Only when you retrace your steps, turning into the congested, narrow lanes to the south of the highway, do you discover the pueblo of your imagination. It is like an archaeological treasure buried beneath new buildings, hidden around the corners of treacherously winding roads, quietly playing second fiddle to the beckoning marquee of the video store. Like their ancestors, who built that older town on the site of a still older one when they left the mountain retreat they inhabited during the Pueblo Uprising, the Zunis have layered new forms onto old foundations, built the present upon the past. Like Dilsey in William Faulkner's *The Sound and the Fury*, they endured.

NOTES

—*☙☙*—

A Preface

1. Shaun Reno, "The Zuni Indian Tribe: A Model for *Stranger in a Strange Land*'s Martian Culture," *Extrapolation*, vol. 36, no. 2 (Summer 1995), pp. 151–59.

1. Finding Zuni

1. See Ronald Takaki, "*The Tempest* in the Wilderness: The Racialization of Savagery," *The Journal of American History*, vol. 79, no. 3 (December 1992), pp. 892–912.
2. See C. Gregory Crampton, *The Zunis of Cibola* (Salt Lake City: University of Utah Press, 1977), pp. 13–15; and T. J. Ferguson and E. Richard Hart, *A Zuni Atlas* (Norman: University of Oklahoma Press, 1985), p. 29.
3. Will Roscoe, *The Zuni Man-Woman* (Albuquerque: University of New Mexico Press, 1991), pp. 13, 17, 152.
4. See Richard Wightman Fox and T. J. Jackson Lears, eds., *The Culture of Consumption: Critical Essays in American History, 1880–1980* (New York: Pantheon, 1983), p. xi.
5. Dennis Tedlock has included a beautiful modern version of this story in *Finding the Center: Narrative Poetry of the Zuni Indians* (New York: Dial Press, 1972). My summary is based on that version.

6. Frank Hamilton Cushing, "Outlines of Zuni Creation Myths," *Bureau of American Ethnology Annual Report for 1891–92* (Washington, D.C.: Government Printing Office, 1896), p. 325.

7. Ibid., p. 342. Cushing also hypothesized an even earlier history, in which the cliff dwellers were chased south to the desert by stronger foes.

8. Ibid., p. 343.

9. Ibid., pp. 355–58, 361–63, 365.

10. Ibid., p. 366.

11. Ibid., p. 350.

12. Ibid., pp. 352–55.

2. Imagining America

1. Frank Hamilton Cushing, "Supplement to Annual Report on Fieldwork for Year Ending June 30, 1883." MS, Cushing Papers, National Anthropological Archives, Smithsonian Institution (hereafter cited as NAA).

2. Simon Bronner, "Object Lessons: The Work of Ethnological Museums and Collections," in Bronner, ed., *Consuming Visions: Accumulation and Display of Goods in America, 1880–1920* (New York: W. W. Norton, 1989), pp. 217, 238. See also Steven Conn, *Museums and American Intellectual Life, 1876–1926* (Chicago: University of Chicago Press, 1998), pp. 3–31.

3. Concerns with the inadequacy of the term "Progressive" to describe this period have been summarized by Peter Filene, "An Obituary for the 'Progressive Movement,'" *American Quarterly*, vol. 22, no. 1 (Spring 1970), but the problem of how, then, to characterize the period has not yet been settled. Robert Wiebe's *The Search for Order, 1877–1920* (New York: Hill & Wang, 1967) has provided a more flexible, inclusive epigram for the period, and historians have fastened on his characterization of the period as one obsessed with order because fearful of its opposite. This characterization, though extremely useful, still focuses only incidentally on the working classes and doesn't really confront the influence of consumer culture, an issue that historians have increasingly investigated in the decades since Wiebe's book was first published.

4. John Higham, "The Reorientation of American Culture in the

1890s," in John Weiss, ed., *The Origins of Modern Consciousness* (Detroit: Wayne State University Press, 1965), pp. 25–33; Burton Bledstein, *The Culture of Professionalism: The Middle Class and the Development of Higher Education in America* (New York: W. W. Norton, 1976), pp. 57–61; and Thomas L. Haskell, *The Emergence of Professional Social Science: The American Social Science Association and the Nineteenth-Century Crisis of Authority* (Urbana: University of Illinois Press, 1977), pp. 38–43.

5. Curtis M. Hinsley, Jr., "Zunis and Brahmins: Cultural Ambivalence in the Gilded Age," in George W. Stocking, Jr., ed., *Romantic Motives: Essays on Anthropological Sensibility* (Madison: University of Wisconsin Press, 1989), pp. 177–78.

6. An excellent study of this early period in anthropology is Robert E. Bieder, *Science Encounters the Indian, 1820–1880: The Early Years of American Ethnology* (Norman: University of Oklahoma Press, 1986).

7. Neil Harris, *Cultural Excursions: Marketing Appetites and Cultural Tastes in Modern America* (Chicago: University of Chicago Press, 1990), p. 271.

3. Two-fold One-Kind: Matilda Stevenson

1. See Will Roscoe, *The Zuni Man-Woman* (Albuquerque: University of New Mexico Press, 1991), pp. 56–57.

2. Ibid., pp. 61–62.

3. Ibid., pp. 55–56, 58–59, 70–71.

4. Ibid., p. 151.

5. Nancy J. Parezo, "Matilda Coxe Evans Stevenson," in Ute Gacs et al., eds., *Women Anthropologists: A Biographical Dictionary* (New York: Greenwood Press, 1988), p. 337.

6. Matilda Stevenson, *The Zuñi Indians: Their Mythology, Esoteric Fraternities, and Ceremonies* (Glorieta, New Mexico: Rio Grande Press, 1970; originally published as *Twenty-third Annual Report of the Bureau of American Ethnology for 1901–1902* in 1904), pp. 16–17; Frank Hamilton Cushing, *My Adventures in Zuñi* (Palmer Lake, Colorado: Filter Press, 1967; originally published in *The Century* magazine, 1882–1883), p. 14; and Parezo, "Matilda Coxe Evans Stevenson," p. 338.

7. Cushing, *My Adventures in Zuñi*, pp. 1, 5, 9, 14.

8. Ibid., p. 9; Stevenson, *The Zuñi Indians*, pp. 16–17, 250; Tilly E. Stevenson, *Zuñi and the Zuñians* (Washington, D.C.: privately printed, 1881); and F. H. Cushing to Spencer Baird, November 24, 1879, reprinted in Jesse Green, ed., *Cushing at Zuni: The Correspondence and Journals of Frank Hamilton Cushing, 1879–1884* (Albuquerque: University of New Mexico Press, 1990), pp. 64–65.

9. Stevenson, *Zuñi and the Zuñians*, pp. 1–2.

10. Ibid., p. 3.

11. Ibid., pp. 5–6.

12. See Lewis Henry Morgan, "The 'Seven Cities of Cibola,' " *North American Review*, vol. 108 (April 1869), pp. 457–98; and Stevenson, *Zuñi and the Zuñians*, p. 27.

13. Stevenson, *Zuñi and the Zuñians*, pp. 12, 23, 29, photograph opposite p. 22; Parezo, "Matilda Coxe Evans Stevenson," p. 338.

14. Stevenson, *Zuñi and the Zuñians*, p. 1.

15. Parezo, "Matilda Coxe Evans Stevenson," p. 339. Stevenson's works on Zuni include "Religious Life of the Zuñi Child," *Fifth Annual Report of the Bureau of American Ethnology for 1883–1884* (Washington, D.C.: Government Printing Office, 1887), pp. 533–55; "Zuñi Religion," *Science*, vol. 11 (1888), pp. 136–37; "A Chapter in Zuñi Mythology," in C. Staniland Wake, ed., *Memoirs of the International Congress of Anthropology* (Chicago, 1894), pp. 312–19; "The Zuñi Scalp Ceremonial," in Mary Kavanaugh O. Eagle, ed., *The Congress of Women* (Chicago: American Publishing House, 1894), pp. 484–87; "Zuñi Ancestral Gods and Masks," *American Anthropologist*, o.s., vol. 11 (1898), pp. 33–40; "Zuñi Games," *American Anthropologist*, n.s., vol. 5 (1903), pp. 468–97; and *The Zuñi Indians*.

16. Nancy Oestreich Lurie, "Women in Early American Anthropology," in June Helm [McNeish], ed., *Pioneers of American Anthropology: The Uses of Biography* (Seattle: University of Washington Press, 1966), pp. 35–38, 58–61; Neil M. Judd, *The Bureau of American Ethnology: A Partial History* (Norman: University of Oklahoma Press, 1967) p. 57; and Parezo, "Matilda Coxe Evans Stevenson," pp. 340–41.

17. Roscoe, *The Zuni Man-Woman*, p. 70.

18. Stevenson, *The Zuñi Indians*, pp. 297–303, 311–13.

19. Judd, *The Bureau of American Ethnology*, p. 57; Parezo, "Matilda Coxe Evans Stevenson," p. 341.

20. Edward B. Tylor, "How the Problems of American Anthropology Present Themselves to the English Mind" (lecture delivered before the Anthropological Society of Washington, October 11, 1884; reprinted in *Science*, vol. 4, 1884), pp. 545–50.

21. Stevenson, *The Zuñi Indians*, p. 250; Lurie, "Women in Early American Anthropology," pp. 59–60.

22. See Stevenson to J. B. Clayton, February 20, 1907; and Stevenson to William Henry Holmes, April 8, April 20, April 22, 1904; February 4, 1907. Stevenson Papers, NAA.

23. Stevenson, *The Zuñi Indians*, pp. 41–43.

24. Lurie, "Women in Early American Anthropology," pp. 58–62; Parezo, "Matilda Coxe Evans Stevenson," p. 339; Stevenson to W. H. Holmes, January 2, 1907, Stevenson Papers, NAA; and Stevenson, *The Zuñi Indians*, pp. 185, 191, and publisher's preface, unpaged.

25. Stevenson, *The Zuñi Indians*, pp. 295–96.

26. Ibid., pp. 294–303.

27. Lurie, "Women in Early American Anthropology," pp. 58–59; W. H. Holmes, "In Memoriam," *American Anthropologist*, n.s., vol. 18, no. 4 (October–December 1916), p. 557.

28. Roscoe, *The Zuni Man-Woman*, pp. 46–52, 120–21.

29. Fred Eggan and T. N. Pandey, "Zuni History, 1850–1970," in Alfonso Ortiz, ed., *Southwest*, vol. 9 of William C. Sturtevant, ed., *Handbook of North American Indians* (Washington, D.C.: Smithsonian Institution Press, 1979), p. 474.

30. Roscoe, *The Zuni Man-Woman*, pp. 31, 120–21; Stevenson, *The Zuñi Indians*, p. 37.

31. See Stevenson, *The Zuñi Indians*, pp. 310–11; Roscoe, *The Zuni Man-Woman*, pp. 46, 52, 53–73; and Edmund Wilson, *Red, Black, Blond and Olive: Studies in Four Civilizations: Zuni, Haiti, Soviet Russia, Israel* (New York: Oxford University Press, 1956), pp. 19–21.

32. Roscoe, *The Zuni Man-Woman*, pp. 44–47, 120; Stevenson, *The Zuñi Indians*, p. 380.

33. Stevenson, *The Zuñi Indians*, pp. 130, 379–83.

34. Ibid.; Lurie, "Women in Early American Anthropology," pp. 55–56.

35. Stevenson, *The Zuñi Indians*, pp. 227–28; Wilson, *Red, Black, Blond and Olive*, pp. 19–21; and Roscoe, *The Zuni Man-Woman*, pp. 104–9.

36. Roscoe, *The Zuni Man-Woman*, pp. 63–65.

37. Ibid.
38. Ibid., pp. 64–66.
39. Ibid.
40. Ibid., pp. 120–22.

4. A Place of Grace: Frank Hamilton Cushing

1. There is no full-length biography of Frank Hamilton Cushing, but several historians of anthropology have written about him in shorter works. The most prolific is Curtis M. Hinsley, Jr., who included an extended discussion in his *Savages and Scientists: The Smithsonian Institution and the Development of American Anthropology, 1846–1910* (Washington, D.C.: Smithsonian Institution Press, 1981). Hinsley is also the author of "Ethnographic Charisma and Scientific Routine," in George W. Stocking, Jr., ed., *Observers Observed: Essays on Ethnographic Fieldwork* (Madison: University of Wisconsin Press, 1983); and "Zunis and Brahmins: Cultural Ambivalence in the Gilded Age," in George W. Stocking, Jr., ed., *Romantic Motives: Essays on Anthropological Sensibility* (Madison: University of Wisconsin Press, 1989), both of which focus on Cushing. Cushing is one of the four anthropologists profiled by Joan Mark in *Four Anthropologists: An American Science in Its Early Years* (New York: Science History Publications, 1980). Jesse Green, too, has woven a biographical narrative through the collections of Cushing's writings he has edited. They include *Zuni: Selected Writings of Frank Hamilton Cushing* (Lincoln: University of Nebraska Press, 1979); and *Cushing at Zuni: The Correspondence and Journals of Frank Hamilton Cushing, 1879–1884* (Albuquerque: University of New Mexico Press, 1990).
2. Marvin Harris, *The Rise of Anthropological Theory*, pp. 145–46, 150, 171; Hinsley, *Savages and Scientists*, pp. 103–5.
3. See Hinsley, *Savages and Scientists*, pp. 202–4; see also Green, ed., *Cushing at Zuni*, p. 26; and *Zuni: Selected Writings*, p. 25 n. 5.
4. W. H. Holmes, "In Memoriam," *American Anthropologist*, n.s., vol. 2, no. 2 (April–June 1900), pp. 354–80.
5. Ibid., pp. 356–57.
6. Ibid., pp. 356–58.
7. Ibid., pp. 358–59.
8. Ibid., pp. 359–60.

9. "Remarks by J. W. Powell," *American Anthropologist*, n.s., vol. 2, no. 2 (April–June 1900), pp. 361.

10. A plaintive, self-justificatory note runs through much of Cushing's correspondence: see Cushing to Spencer Baird, November 7, 1879, reprinted in Green, ed., *Cushing at Zuni*, pp. 60–62. See also Green's editorial note, p. 320, and a piece Cushing probably authored in the *Boston Herald*, April 20, 1884, pp. 321–22.

11. The three-part series, published in December 1882, February 1883, and May 1883 in *The Century*, has been reprinted as a booklet, from which I take my citations. Frank Hamilton Cushing, *My Adventures in Zuñi* (Palmer Lake, Colorado: Filter Press, 1967). Cushing's publications previous to this were "The Zuñi Social, Mythic, and Religious Systems," *Popular Science Monthly*, vol. 21 (June 1882); and "The Nation of the Willows," *Atlantic Monthly*, vol. 50 (September and October 1882). That Cushing compressed his experiences to fit in the cycle of a single year is suggested by Jesse Green in *Zuni: Selected Writings*, p. 38.

12. Cushing, *My Adventures in Zuñi*, pp. 1–2.

13. Ibid.

14. The tone of much of Cushing's writing suggests that he was a lone white man entirely surrounded by Indians. In fact, white missionaries and traders show up periodically in his accounts, and some of them apparently lived at or near Zuni. See ibid., pp. 9, 14.

15. Ibid., pp. 2–3.

16. Ibid., p. 2.

17. Ibid., pp. 2–4.

18. Ibid., pp. 7–8.

19. Ibid., p. 5.

20. Ibid., p. 9. Green, in editorial notes in *Cushing at Zuni*, p. 38, suggests that though in later memoirs Cushing remembered moving into the governor's house after a few weeks, his writings at the time indicate a much shorter period.

21. See Cushing, *My Adventures in Zuñi*, p. 9; and Cushing, "Life in Zuni" (lecture delivered in Buffalo, New York, December 10, 1890, in Green, *Cushing at Zuni*), p. 40.

22. Green, ed., *Cushing at Zuni*, pp. 4, 40.

23. Cushing, *My Adventures in Zuñi*, pp. 10–11.

24. Ibid., pp. 41–43.

25. Ibid., pp. 12–13.

26. Ibid., pp. 18, 28–29.

27. See, for example, Cushing, "A Study of Pueblo Pottery, As Illustrative of Zuñi Culture Growth," *Bureau of American Ethnology Annual Report for 1883* (Washington, D.C.: Government Printing Office, 1886), pp. 471–521; and Cushing, "Outlines of Zuñi Creation Myths," *Bureau of American Ethnology Annual Report for 1891–1892* (Washington, D.C.: Government Printing Office, 1896), pp. 325–447.

28. See T. J. Jackson Lears, *No Place of Grace: Antimodernism and the Transformation of American Culture, 1880–1920* (New York: Pantheon Books, 1981), p. 23.

29. Cushing's campaign to learn the secrets of the kivas makes up a central part of *My Adventures in Zuñi*. He recorded his travels into the countryside in search of other sacred places in letters and journals, many of which have been collected by Jesse Green in *Cushing at Zuni*.

30. Descriptions of these public ceremonies were the mainstay of anthropological writings on Zuni. Cushing's first encounter with the Zunis, at least as he recorded it for his *Century* articles, occurred during one such ceremony. Cushing, *My Adventures in Zuñi*, pp. 2–5.

31. Will Roscoe, *The Zuni Man-Woman* (Albuquerque: University of New Mexico Press, 1991), p. 17. The most comprehensive source on Zuni's secret societies is Matilda Stevenson's *The Zuñi Indians*.

32. See Stevenson's description of the "Quadrennial Dance of the Kia'nakwe," in *The Zuñi Indians*, pp. 217–26; Green, ed., *Cushing at Zuni*, pp. 66–84; and Roscoe, *The Zuni Man-Woman*, pp. 50–51.

33. The suggestion that Cushing engaged in a series of reciprocating exchanges with the Zunis, in effect forcing them to initiate him, comes from Green, ed., *Cushing at Zuni*, pp. 6–8.

34. Ibid., pp. 38–39, 361 n. 31; Cushing, *My Adventures in Zuñi*, pp. 21–22.

35. Cushing, *My Adventures in Zuñi*, pp. 31–33.

36. Ibid., pp. 23, 32.

37. Ibid., p. 32.

38. Hinsley, "Zunis and Brahmins," pp. 182–84.

39. In recent years the Zunis have made efforts to repatriate their gods and some of the prayer plumes that anthropologists, wittingly or

not, stole from them. The American Museum of Natural History in New York returned one war god in 1990, which the Zunis planned to place in a secure but open outdoor site to deteriorate naturally. See "Transfer of War God Material to the Zuni," American Museum of Natural History accession report no. 1916–65.
40. Stewart Culin, "The Treasure Cave of the Little Fire," MS, Culin Papers, Brooklyn Museum of Art Archives.
41. Green, ed., *Cushing at Zuni*, pp. 66–86, 330–32.
42. Cushing, "A Study of Pueblo Pottery," pp. 482–93.
43. Ibid., pp. 510–11.
44. Ibid.
45. See Ruth Benedict, *Patterns of Culture* (Boston: Houghton Mifflin, 1934), pp. 113–14.
46. Cushing, *My Adventures in Zuñi*, pp. 44–45; Green, ed., *Cushing at Zuni*, pp. 11, 13–14, 116, 129–30; and Hinsley, *Savages and Scientists*, pp. 196–97.
47. See Neil M. Judd, *The Bureau of American Ethnology: A Partial History* (Norman: University of Oklahoma Press, 1967), p. 60; Green, ed., *Cushing at Zuni*, pp. 178, 181; and Stewart Culin, "Zuñi Pictures," in Elsie Clews Parsons, ed., *American Indian Life by Several of Its Students* (New York: B. W. Heubsch, 1922), p. 175.
48. Frank Hamilton Cushing, "Life in Zuñi," in Green, ed., *Zuni: Selected Writings*. See also Green, ed., *Cushing at Zuni*, pp. 153–56, 181–82, 354n.
49. Cushing, *My Adventures in Zuñi*, p. 27; Roscoe, *The Zuni Man-Woman*, p. 128.
50. Green, ed., *Cushing at Zuni*, pp. 7, 361n; Cushing, "A Study of Pueblo Pottery," pp. 473–521.

5. Blue Beard's Chamber: Stewart Culin

1. See "Culin's Private Report to Institute Directors," *The Brooklyn Daily Eagle*, February 26, 1904; and Stewart Culin, "Guide to the Southwestern Indian Hall," *Brooklyn Institute of Arts and Sciences, The Museum News*, vol. 2 (April 1907), p. 105. See also Ira Jacknis, "The Road to Beauty," in Diana Fane et al., eds., *Objects of Myth and Memory: American Indian Art at the Brooklyn Museum* (New York: Brooklyn Museum, 1991), p. 32.

2. See Jacknis, "The Road to Beauty," pp. 31–32; Stewart Culin, "Report on the Department of Ethnology," *Museum of the Brooklyn Institute of Arts and Sciences, Report for the Year 1905*, photograph between pages 26 and 27; and Culin, "Guide to the Southwestern Indian Hall," pp. 106–7.

3. See Hinsley, *Savages and Scientists*, pp. 97–98; Ira Jacknis, "Franz Boas and Exhibits: On the Limitations of the Museum Method of Anthropology," in George W. Stocking, ed., *Objects and Others: Essays on Museums and Material Culture* (Madison: University of Wisconsin Press, 1985), pp. 90–91.

4. See Jacknis, "The Road to Beauty," pp. 30, 35; and "Franz Boas and Exhibits," pp. 95–103.

5. Frank Hamilton Cushing to Stewart Culin, October 7, 1894. Culin Papers, Brooklyn Museum Archives.

6. See "Culin's Private Report to Institute Directors"; and Jacknis, "The Road to Beauty," p. 32.

7. "A Zuni Exhibit," *The Evening Post*, May 31, 1905; "Museum Opens Exhibit of American Ethnology," *The Brooklyn Daily Eagle*, June 2, 1905.

8. "Museum Opens Exhibit of American Ethnology"; Diana Fane, "The Language of Things," in Fane et al., eds., *Objects of Myth and Memory*, p. 26.

9. Fane, "The Language of Things," p. 14; Simon J. Bronner, "Object Lessons: The Work of Ethnological Museums and Collections," in Bronner, ed., *Consuming Visions: Accumulation and Display of Goods in America, 1880–1920* (New York: W. W. Norton, 1989), pp. 217–54.

10. Stewart Culin, "Creation in Art," *The Brooklyn Museum Quarterly*, vol. 11, no. 3, (1924), p. 96.

11. Fane, "The Language of Things," pp. 14–15.

12. Stewart Culin, "A Visit to the Indians of New Mexico and Arizona, 1902," Culin Papers, Brooklyn Museum of Art Archives.

13. Stewart Culin, "Zuñi Pictures," in Elsie Clews Parsons, ed., *American Indian Life by Several of Its Students* (New York: B. W. Huebsch, 1922), pp. 175–78.

14. Culin, "Zuñi Pictures," p. 175.

15. Stewart Culin, "Pictures of Travel," MS, Culin Papers, Brooklyn Museum of Art Archives.

16. Culin, "Zuñi Pictures," p. 175.

17. Ibid., p. 176.
18. Ibid., pp. 176–77.
19. Ibid., pp. 177–78.
20. Culin, "A Visit to the Indians of New Mexico and Arizona, 1902," Culin Papers, Brooklyn Museum of Art Archives, p. 13.
21. Ibid., p. 14.
22. Culin, "Collecting Trip Among the Indians of the Southwest, 1904," Culin Papers, Brooklyn Museum of Art Archives, p. 22.
23. Culin, "A Visit to the Indians of New Mexico and Arizona, 1902," p. 4.
24. Culin, "Collecting Trip Among the Indians of the Southwest, 1903," Culin Papers, Brooklyn Museum of Art Archives, pp. 31–32, 89.
25. Stewart Culin, "The Treasure Cave of the Little Fire," pp. 1, 5; and "Blue Beard's Chamber," p. 1. Both MSS in Culin Papers, Brooklyn Museum of Art Archives.
26. Culin, "Collecting Trip Among the Indians of the Southwest, 1903," pp. 32, 47–48.
27. Culin, "Blue Beard's Chamber," pp. 3–4.
28. Ibid., pp. 8–9.
29. Culin, "Collecting Trip Among the Indians of the Southwest, 1904," pp. 9–10.
30. Ibid., pp. 23; Fane et al., eds., *Objects of Myth and Memory*, pp. 142–43.
31. Culin, "Collecting Trip Among the Indians of the Southwest, 1904," pp. 23–28.
32. Ibid., pp. 28–31.
33. Culin, "Collecting Trip Among the Indians of New Mexico and California, 1907," Culin Papers, Brooklyn Museum of Art Archives; Culin, "A Visit to the Indians of New Mexico and Arizona, 1902," p. 16.
34. Culin, "Collecting Trip Among the Indians of New Mexico and California," p. 162.
35. Ibid., pp. 162, 176; Culin, "A Visit to the Indians of New Mexico and Arizona, 1902," p. 3.
36. Culin, "Collecting Trip Among the Indians of New Mexico and California, 1907," p. 184.
37. This and subsequent references are to Culin, "The Treasure Cave of the Little Fire."

38. See Fane, "The Language of Things," pp. 21–25.
39. Ibid., pp. 18, 23.
40. See Jacknis, "The Road to Beauty," p. 32.
41. See Fane, "The Language of Things," p. 23; and Jacknis, "The Road to Beauty," pp. 31, 36. In 1919 Culin, Herbert Spindon, from the American Museum of Natural History, and an editor of *Women's Wear Daily* named Morris Crawford put together an exhibit showing the influence museum ethnology exhibits had had on fashion designers. See Jacknis, "The Road to Beauty," p. 42.
42. See Jacknis, "The Road to Beauty," pp. 37–38.
43. Stewart Culin, "The Road to Beauty," *The Brooklyn Museum Quarterly*, vol. 14, no. 2 (April 1927), p. 44.
44. Ibid., pp. 43, 46.
45. Ibid., pp. 41–49.

6. Conclusion: Zuni Legacy

1. See Jesse Green, ed., *Cushing at Zuni: The Correspondence and Journals of Frank Hamilton Cushing, 1879–1884* (Albuquerque: University of New Mexico Press, 1990), pp. 14, 18; and Curtis M. Hinsley, Jr., *Savages and Scientists: The Smithsonian Institution and the Development of American Anthropology, 1846–1910* (Washington, D.C.: Smithsonian Institution Press, 1981), pp. 200–5.
2. See Nancy J. Parezo, "Matilda Coxe Evans Stevenson," in Ute Gacs et al., eds., *Women Anthropologists: A Biographical Dictionary* (New York: Greenwood Press, 1988), pp. 340–41; Nancy Oestreich Lurie, "Women in Early American Anthropology," in June Helm [McNeish], ed., *Pioneers of American Anthropology: The Uses of Biography* (Seattle: University of Washington Press, 1966), p. 64; Stewart Culin, "Expedition Report for 1907," Culin Papers, Brooklyn Museum, p. 184; Rosemary Levy Zumwalt, *Wealth and Rebellion: Elsie Clews Parsons, Anthropologist and Folklorist* (Urbana: University of Illinois Press, 1992), p. 211; and Margaret Lewis to Elsie Clews Parsons, September 25 (no year given). Parsons Papers, American Philosophical Society, Philadelphia (hereafter cited as APS).
3. See Clark Wissler, "General Introduction," "The Archer M. Huntington Survey of the Southwest Zuni District," *Anthropological Papers of the American Museum of Natural History*, vol. 18 (1919), pp. iii, vi.

4. See ibid., pp. iii, vi; Zumwalt, *Wealth and Rebellion*, pp. 152, 176; Elsie Clews Parsons to Herbert Parsons, August 7, 1915, August 13, 1915; Franz Boas to Elsie Clews Parsons, November 24, 1915, July 3, 1919, July 9, 1920, July 23, 1921, June 12, 1924; Ruth Benedict to Elsie Clews Parsons, June 19, 1937; and Elsie Clews Parsons to Franz Boas, June 18, 1929. Parsons Papers, APS.

5. Zumwalt, *Wealth and Rebellion*, pp. 211–12.

6. Franz Boas, "The Occurrence of Similar Inventions in Areas Widely Apart," *Science*, vol. 9, no. 224 (May 20, 1887), pp. 485–86; Boas, untitled, *Science*, vol. 9, no. 228 (June 17, 1887), pp. 587–89.

7. Alfred L. Kroeber to Elsie Clews Parsons, October 18, 1923. Parsons Papers, APS.

8. See Christopher M. Lyman, *The Vanishing Race and Other Illusions: Photographs of Indians by Edward S. Curtis* (Washington, D.C.: Smithsonian Institution Press, 1982), p. 63 and passim; and Lurie, "Women in Early American Anthropology," p. 61.

9. Ruth Benedict, *Patterns of Culture* (Boston: Houghton Mifflin, 1934, reprinted 1989), pp. 57–129; Stewart Culin, "The Road to Beauty," *Brooklyn Museum Quarterly*, vol. 14, no. 2 (April 1927), pp. 43–44, 48; and Curtis Hinsley, Jr., "Zunis and Brahmins: Cultural Ambivalence in the Gilded Age," in George W. Stocking, Jr., ed., *Romantic Motives: Essays on Anthropological Sensibility* (Madison: University of Wisconsin Press, 1989), pp. 182–83.

10. See Triloki Nath Pandey, "Anthropologists at Zuni," *Proceedings of the American Philosophical Society*, vol. 116 (1972), pp. 321–37.

11. See Brian W. Dippie, *The Vanishing American: White Attitudes and U.S. Indian Policy* (Middletown, Conn.: Wesleyan University Press, 1982), pp. 228–34.

12. See Daniel G. Brinton, " 'The Nation' as an Element in Anthropology," in C. Staniland Wake, ed., *Memoirs of the International Congress of Anthropology* (Chicago: Schulte, 1894), pp. 19–34; and Barbara Kirshenblatt-Gimblett, "Objects of Ethnography," in Ivan Karp and Steven D. Lavine, eds., *Exhibiting Cultures: The Poetics and Politics of Museum Display* (Washington D.C.: Smithsonian Institution Press, 1991), p. 416.

13. See Dippie, *The Vanishing American*, pp. 106, 167–72.

14. See D. H. Thomas, *The Southwestern Indian Detours: The Story of the Fred Harvey/Santa Fe Railway Experiment in "Detourism"* (Phoenix: Hunter, 1978), pp. 17, 76.

NOTES

15. Marta Weigle, "From Desert to Disney World," *Journal of Anthropological Research*, vol. 45, no. 1 (Spring 1989), pp. 120–25.
16. Benedict, *Patterns of Culture*, pp. 78–79.
17. Warren I. Susman, *Culture as History: The Transformation of American Society in the Twentieth Century* (New York: Pantheon, 1984), pp. 153–54.

BIBLIOGRAPHY

━━◆◆━━

Archives

Brooklyn, New York
Brooklyn Museum of Art Archives:
    Stewart Culin Papers

New York, New York
American Museum of Natural History:
    Anthropology Archives

Philadelphia, Pennsylvania
American Philosophical Society:
    Franz Boas Papers
    Elsie Clews Parsons Papers

Phoenix, Arizona
Heard Museum:
    Fred Harvey Company Papers

Santa Fe, New Mexico
Museum of New Mexico, Historical Section:
    Edgar Lee Hewett Papers

Washington, D.C.
Smithsonian Institution
National Museum of Natural History:
  National Anthropological Archives
  Anthropological Society of Washington Papers
  Bureau of American Ethnology Letterbooks, 1879–1920
  Bureau of American Ethnology Letters Received, 1879–1910
  Matilda Coxe Stevenson Papers
  USNM Papers
  Frank Hamilton Cushing Papers

Works on Zuni

Bandelier, A. F. "Hemenway Southwestern Archaeological Expedition I: Outline of the Documentary History of the Zuni Tribe." *Journal of American Ethnology and Archaeology* 13: 1–115.

Boas, Franz. "Tales of Spanish Provenience from Zuni." *Journal of American Folklore* 35 (1922): 62–98.

Boas, Franz, and Elsie Clews Parsons. "Spanish Tales from Laguna and Zuni, New Mexico." *Journal of American Folklore* 33 (1920): 47–72.

Cozzens, Samuel Woodworth. *The Ancient Cibola: The Marvellous Country; or, Three Years in Arizona and New Mexico.* Boston, 1876.

Crampton, Gregory. *The Zunis of Cibola.* Salt Lake City, 1977.

Culin, Stewart. "Zuñi Pictures." In *American Indian Life by Several of Its Students*, edited by Elsie Clews Parsons, 175–78. New York, 1922.

Cushing, Frank Hamilton. "A Study of Pueblo Pottery, As Illustrative of Zuni Cultural Growth." *Bureau of American Ethnology Annual Report for 1883*: 467–521.

———. *My Adventures in Zuñi.* Palmer Lake, Colo., 1967.

———. "Outlines of Zuni Creation Myths." *Bureau of American Ethnology Annual Report for 1891–92*: 325–447.

———. "Primitive Copper Working: An Experimental Study." *American Anthropologist* 7 (1894): 93–117.

———. "The Nation of the Willows." *Atlantic Monthly* 50 (1882): 274–362, 541–59.

———. "The Zuni Social, Mythic, and Religious Systems." *Popular Science Monthly* 21 (1882): 189–92.

————. *Zuni Breadstuff.* New York, 1920.

————. "Zuni Fetiches." *Bureau of American Ethnology Annual Report for 1880–81*: 3–45.

————. *Zuni Folk Tales.* New York, 1901 (reissued 1931).

Fergusson, Erna. *Dancing Gods: Indian Ceremonials of New Mexico and Arizona.* Albuquerque, 1931.

Fewkes, J. Walter. "A Few Summer Ceremonials at Zuni Pueblo." *Journal of American Ethnology and Archaeology* 1 (1891): 1–62.

Gillman, Benjamin Ives. "Zuni Melodies." *Journal of American Ethnology and Archaeology* 1 (1891): 63–91.

Green, Jesse, ed. *Cushing at Zuni: The Correspondence and Journals of Frank Hamilton Cushing, 1879–1884.* Albuquerque, 1990.

————, ed. *Zuni: Selected Writings of Frank Hamilton Cushing.* Lincoln, 1979.

Kintigh, Keith W. *Settlement, Subsistence and Society in Late Zuni Prehistory.* Tucson, 1985.

Klett, Francis. "The Zuni Indians of New Mexico." *Popular Science Monthly* 5 (1874): 580–91.

Kroeber, A. L. "The Oldest Town in America and Its People." *American Museum Journal* 16 (1916): 81–86.

————. "Zuni Kin and Clan." *Anthropological Papers of the American Museum of Natural History* 18, pt. 2 (1917): 47–205.

————. "Zuni Potsherds." *Anthropological Papers of the American Museum of Natural History* 18, pt. 1 (1917): 1–37.

Leighton, Dorothea C., and John Adair. *People of the Middle Place: A Study of the Zuni Indians.* New Haven, 1966.

Li An-Che. "Zuni: Some Observations and Queries." *American Anthropologist* 39 (1937): 62–76.

Morgan, Lewis Henry. "The 'Seven Cities of Cibola.' " *North American Review* 108 (1869): 457–98.

Pandey, T. N. "Anthropologists at Zuni." *Proceedings of the American Philosophical Society* 116 (1972): 321–37.

Parsons, Elsie Clews. "A Few Zuni Death Beliefs and Practices." *American Anthropologist,* n.s., 18 (1916): 245–56.

————. "Nativity Myth at Laguna and Zuni." *Journal of American Folklore* 31 (1918): 256–63.

————. "Notes on Zuni." *Memoirs of the American Anthropological Association* 4, pts. 3 and 4 (1917): 151–327.

————. "Pueblo-Indian Folk-tales, Probably of Spanish Provenience." *Journal of American Folklore* 31 (1918): 216–55.

———. "The Origin Myth of Zuni." *Journal of American Folklore* 36 (1923): 135–62.

———. "The Scalp Ceremonial of Zuni." *Memoirs of the American Anthropological Association* 31 (1924): entire.

Pueblo of Zuni. *The Zunis: Experiences and Descriptions.* Salt Lake City, 1973.

Quam, Alvina, trans. *The Zunis: Self-Portrayals by the Zuni People.* Albuquerque, 1972.

Roscoe, Will. *The Zuni Man-Woman.* Albuquerque, 1991.

Stevenson, Matilda Coxe. "A Chapter in Zuñi Mythology." In *Memoirs of the International Congress of Anthropology,* edited by C. Staniland Wake, 312–19. Chicago, 1894.

———. "Ethnobotany of the Zuñi Indians." *Bureau of American Ethnology Annual Report for 1908–1909*: 35–102.

———. "Religious Life of the Zuñi Child." Fifth Annual Report of the *Bureau of American Ethnology Annual Report for 1883–1884*: 533–55.

———. *The Zuñi Indians: Their Mythology, Esoteric Fraternities and Ceremonies.* Glorieta, N. Mex., 1970.

———. "The Zuñi Scalp Ceremonial." In *The Congress of Women,* edited by Mary Kavanaugh O. Eagle, 484–87. Chicago, 1894.

———. "Zuñi Ancestral Gods and Masks." *American Anthropologist,* o.s., 11 (1898): 33–40.

———. *Zuñi and the Zuñians.* Washington, D.C., 1881.

———. "Zuñi Games." *American Anthropologist,* n.s., 5 (1903): 468–97.

———. "Zuñi Religion." *Science* 11 (1888): 136–37.

General Works

Babcock, Barbara A., and Nancy J. Parezo. *Daughters of the Desert: Women Anthropologists and the Native American Southwest, 1880–1980.* Albuquerque, 1988.

Bederman, Gail. *Manliness and Civilization: A Cultural History of Gender and Race in the United States, 1880–1917.* Chicago, 1995.

Bell, Whitfield J., ed. *A Cabinet of Curiosities: Five Episodes in the Evolution of American Museums.* Charlottesville, 1967.

Benedict, Burton, et al. *The Anthropology of World's Fairs: San Francisco Panama-Pacific International Exposition, 1915.* Berkeley, 1983.

Benedict, Ruth. *Patterns of Culture.* Boston, 1934.

Berkhofer, Robert F. *The White Man's Indian: Images of the American Indian from Columbus to the Present.* New York, 1978.

Berman, Marshall. *All That Is Solid Melts into Air.* New York, 1982.

Bieder, Robert E. *Science Encounters the Indian, 1820–1880: The Early Years of American Ethnology.* Norman, Okla., 1986.

Bledstein, Burton. *The Culture of Professionalism: The Middle Class and the Development of Higher Education in America.* New York, 1976.

Bogdan, Robert. *Freak Show: Presenting Human Oddities for Amusement and Profit.* Chicago, 1988.

Boyer, Paul. *Urban Masses and Moral Order in America, 1820–1920.* Cambridge, Mass., 1978.

Brinton, Daniel G. *Essays of an Americanist.* Philadelphia, 1890.

Bronner, Simon J., ed. *Consuming Visions: Accumulation and Display of Goods in America, 1880–1920.* New York, 1989.

Chandler, Alfred D. *The Visible Hand: The Managerial Revolution in American Business.* Cambridge, Mass., 1977.

Chauvenet, Beatrice. *Hewett and Friends: A Biography of Santa Fe's Vibrant Era.* Santa Fe, 1983.

Clifford, James. *The Predicament of Culture: Twentieth-Century Ethnography, Literature and Art.* Cambridge, Mass., 1988.

Clifford, James, and George Marcus. *Writing Culture: The Poetics and Politics of Ethnography.* Berkeley, 1986.

Cole, Douglas. *Captured Heritage: The Scramble for Northwest Coast Artifacts.* Seattle, 1985.

Cotkin, George. *Reluctant Modernism: American Thought and Culture, 1880–1900.* Boston, 1991.

Curtis, William E. *Children of the Sun.* Chicago, 1883.

Degler, Carl. *In Search of Human Nature: The Decline and Revival of Darwinism in American Social Thought.* New York, 1991.

Dippie, Brian W. *The Vanishing American: White Attitudes and U.S. Indian Policy.* Middletown, Conn., 1982.

Dorsey, George A. *Indians of the Southwest.* 1903.

Douglas, Mary, and Baron Isherwood. *The World of Goods.* New York, 1979.

Drinnon, Richard. *Facing West: The Metaphysics of Indian-Hating and Empire-Building.* Minneapolis, 1980.

Dupree, A. Hunter. *Science in the Federal Government: A History of Policies and Activities to 1940.* Cambridge, Mass., 1957.

Ehrenreich, Barbara, and John Ehrenreich. "The Professional Managerial Class." In *Between Labor and Capital*, edited by Pat Walker, 5–45. Boston, 1979.

Fabian, Johannes. *Time and the Other: How Anthropology Makes Its Object*. New York, 1983.

Fane, Diana, et al., eds. *Objects of Myth and Memory: American Indian Art at the Brooklyn Museum*. New York, 1991.

Fox, Richard Wightman, and T. J. Jackson Lears, eds., *The Culture of Consumption: Critical Essays in American History, 1880–1980*. New York, 1983.

Furner, Mary O. *Advocacy and Objectivity: A Crisis in the Professionalization of American Social Science, 1865–1905*. Lexington, Ky., 1975.

Gates, Henry Louis, Jr., ed. *"Race," Writing and Difference*. Chicago, 1986.

Geertz, Clifford. *The Interpretation of Cultures*. New York, 1973.

———. *Works and Lives: The Anthropologist as Author*. Stanford, 1988.

Goetzman, William H. *Exploration and Empire: The Explorer and the Scientist in the Winning of the American West*. New York, 1966.

Gossett, Thomas F. *Race: The History of an Idea in America*. New York, 1963.

Gould, Stephen Jay. *The Mismeasure of Man*. New York, 1981.

Graburn, Nelson H. H. *Ethnic and Tourist Arts: Cultural Expressions from the Fourth World*. Berkeley, 1976.

Grattan, Virginia L. *Mary Colter: Builder upon the Red Earth*. Flagstaff, 1980.

Harraway, Donna. *Primate Visions: Gender, Race and Nature in the World of Modern Science*. New York, 1989.

Hale, Grace Elizabeth. *Making Whiteness: The Culture of Segregation in the South, 1890–1940*. New York, 1998.

Hale, Peter Bacon. *Silver Cities: The Photography of American Urbanization*. Philadelphia, 1984.

Hare, Peter H. *A Woman's Quest for Science: Portrait of Anthropologist Elsie Clews Parsons*. New York, 1985.

Harris, Marvin. *The Rise of Anthropological Theory: A History of Theories of Culture*. New York, 1968.

Harris, Neil. *Cultural Excursions: Marketing Appetites and Cultural Tastes in Modern America*. Chicago, 1990.

———. *Humbug: The Art of P. T. Barnum*. Boston, 1973.

Harvey, David. *The Condition of Postmodernity: An Enquiry into the Origins of Cultural Change.* Oxford, Eng., 1990.

Haskell, Thomas L. *The Emergence of Professional Social Science: The American Social Science Association and the Nineteenth-Century Crisis of Authority.* Urbana, Ill., 1977.

Helm, June. *Pioneers of American Anthropology: The Uses of Biography.* Seattle, 1966.

Herbert, Christopher. *Culture and Anomie: Ethnographic Imagination in the Nineteenth Century.* Chicago, 1991.

Herdt, Gilbert, ed. *Third Sex, Third Gender: Beyond Sexual Dimorphism in Culture and History.* New York, 1994.

Higham, John. *Strangers in the Land: Patterns of American Nativism, 1860–1925.* New York, 1985.

Hinsley, Curtis M., Jr. *Savages and Scientists: The Smithsonian Institution and the Development of American Anthropology, 1846–1910.* Washington, D.C., 1981.

Hodge, Frederick W. *Handbook of American Indians North of Mexico.* Washington, D.C., 1907.

Hofstadter, Richard. *Social Darwinism in American Thought.* Boston, 1955.

Horsman, Reginald. *Race and Manifest Destiny.* Cambridge, Mass., 1981.

Hyatt, Marshall. *Franz Boas, Social Activist: The Dynamics of Ethnicity.* New York, 1990.

Jonaitis, Aldona, ed. *Chiefly Feasts: The Enduring Kwakiutl Potlatch.* New York, 1991.

Judd, Neil M. *The Bureau of American Ethnology: A Partial History.* Norman, Okla., 1967.

Karp, Ivan, and Steven D. Lavine, eds. *Exhibiting Cultures: The Poetics and Politics of Museum Display.* Washington, D.C., 1991.

Kern, Stephen. *The Culture of Time and Space, 1880–1918.* Cambridge, Mass., 1983.

Kuhn, Thomas S. *The Structure of Scientific Revolutions.* Chicago, 1970.

Lears, T. J. Jackson. *Fables of Abundance: A Cultural History of Advertising in America.* New York, 1994.

———. *No Place of Grace: Antimodernism and the Transformation of American Culture, 1880–1920.* New York, 1981.

Lefebvre, Henri. *The Production of Space.* Oxford, Eng., 1991.

Limerick, Patricia Nelson. *The Legacy of Conquest: The Unbroken Past of the American West.* New York, 1987.

Lovejoy, Arthur O. *The Great Chain of Being: A Study of the History of an Idea*. Cambridge, Mass., 1936.

MacCannell, David. *The Tourist: A New Theory of the Leisure Class*. New York, 1976.

Manning, Thomas J. *Government in Science: The U.S. Geological Survey, 1867–1894*. Lexington, Ky., 1967.

Mark, Joan. *Four Anthropologists: An American Science in Its Early Years*. New York, 1980.

————. *A Stranger in Her Native Land: Alice Fletcher and the American Indians*. Lincoln, 1988.

McLuhan, T. C. *Dreamtracks: The Railroad and the American Indian, 1893–1930*. New York, 1985.

Mitchell, Lee Clark. *Witnesses to a Vanishing America: The Nineteenth-Century Response*. Princeton, 1981.

Morgan, Lewis Henry. *Ancient Society; or Researches in the Lines of Human Progress from Savagery Through Barbarism to Civilization*. New York, 1877.

Oleson, Alexandra, and John Voss, eds. *The Organization of Knowledge in Modern America, 1860–1920*. Baltimore, 1976.

Ortiz, Alfonso. *New Perspectives on the Pueblos*. Albuquerque, 1972.

Ortiz, Alfonso, ed. *Southwest*, vol. 9 of William C. Sturtevant, ed., *Handbook of North American Indians* 9: 474–81. Washington, D.C., 1979.

Orvell, Miles. *The Real Thing: Imitation and Authenticity in American Culture, 1880–1940*. Chapel Hill, 1989.

Parsons, Elsie Clews, ed. *American Indian Life by Several of Its Students*. New York, 1922.

Pearce, Roy Harvey. *Savagism and Civilization: A Study of the Indian and the American Mind*. Baltimore, 1967.

Powell, John Wesley. *Introduction to the Study of Indian Languages with Words, Phrases and Sentences to be Collected*. Washington, D.C., 1877.

Quimby, I.M.G., ed. *Material Culture and the Study of American Life*. New York, 1978.

Rosenberg, Charles E. *No Other Gods: On Science and American Social Thought*. Baltimore, 1976.

Rosenberg, Rosalind. *Beyond Separate Spheres: Intellectual Roots of Modern Feminism*. New Haven, 1982.

Rossiter, Margaret W. *Women Scientists in America: Struggles and Strategies to 1940.* Baltimore, 1982.

Rydell, Robert W. *All the World's a Fair: Visions of Empire at American International Expositions, 1876–1916.* Chicago, 1984.

Sears, John F. *Sacred Places: American Tourist Attractions in the Nineteenth Century.* New York, 1989.

Slotkin, Richard. *The Fatal Environment: The Myth of the Frontier in the Age of Industrialization, 1800–1890.* New York, 1985.

Smith, Henry Nash. *Virgin Land: The American West as Symbol and Myth.* New York, 1950.

Smith-Rosenberg, Carroll. *Disorderly Conduct: Visions of Gender in Victorian America.* New York, 1986.

Spicer, E. H. *Cycles of Conquest: The Impact of Spain, Mexico, and the United States on the Indians of the Southwest, 1533–1960.* Tucson, 1962.

Stegner, Wallace. *Beyond the Hundredth Meridian: John Wesley Powell and the Second Opening of the West.* Boston, 1954.

Stepan, Nancy Leys. *The Idea of Race in Science: Great Britain, 1800–1900.* Hamden, Conn., 1982.

Stocking, George W., Jr., ed. *Objects and Others: Essays on Museums and Material Culture.* Madison, 1985.

———, ed. *Observers Observed: Essays on Ethnographic Fieldwork.* Madison, 1983.

———, ed. *Race, Culture, and Evolution: Essays in the History of Anthropology.* Chicago, 1982.

———, ed. *Romantic Motives: Essays on Anthropological Sensibility.* Madison, 1989.

———, ed. *The Shaping of American Anthropology, 1883–1911: A Franz Boas Reader.* New York, 1974.

Susman, Warren I. *Culture as History: The Transformation of American Society in the Twentieth Century.* New York, 1984.

Takaki, Ronald T. *Iron Cages: Race and Culture in 19th-Century America.* Seattle, 1982.

Thomas, D. H. *The Southwestern Indian Detours: The Story of the Fred Harvey/Santa Fe Railway Experiment in "Detourism."* Phoenix, 1978.

Wake, C. Staniland, ed. *Memoirs of the International Congress of Anthropology.* Chicago, 1894.

Wallace, Susan E. *The Land of the Pueblos.* New York, 1888.

Wiebe, Robert H. *The Search for Order, 1877–1920.* New York, 1967.

Wilson, Edmund. *Red, Black, Blond and Olive: Studies in Four Civilizations: Zuni, Haiti, Soviet Russia, Israel.* New York, 1956.

Zumwalt, Rosemary Levy. *Wealth and Rebellion: Elsie Clews Parsons, Anthropologist and Folklorist.* Urbana, Ill., 1992.

Zunz, Olivier. *Making America Corporate, 1870–1920.* Chicago, 1990.

Articles and Unpublished Works

Baxter, Sylvester. "An Aboriginal Pilgrimage." *The Century* 24 (1882): 526–36.

———. "F. H. Cushing at Zuni." *American Architect & Building News* 11 (1882): 319.

———. "Mr. Cushing and the Zunis at Washington." *American Architect & Building News* 11 (1882): 121–22.

———. "The Father of the Pueblos." *Harper's New Monthly Magazine,* June 1882: 72–91.

———. "Zuni Revisited." *American Architect & Building News* 13 (1883): 124–26.

Boas, Franz. "Museums of Ethnology and Their Classification." *Science* 9 (1887): 587–89.

Brandes, Raymond Stewart. *Frank Hamilton Cushing: Pioneer Americanist.* Ph.D. diss, University of Arizona, 1965.

Brinton, Daniel. "The 'Nation' as an Element in Anthropology." In *Memoirs of the International Congress of Anthropology,* edited by C. Staniland Wake, 19–34. Chicago, 1894.

Culin, Stewart. *Games of the North American Indians.* New York, 1975.

———. "Guide to the Southwestern Indian Hall." *Brooklyn Institute of Arts and Sciences, The Museum News* 2 (1907): 105–11.

———. "The Road to Beauty." *Brooklyn Museum Quarterly* 14 (1927): 41–50.

Darnell, R. D. *The Development of American Anthropology, 1879–1920: From the Bureau of American Ethnology to Franz Boas.* Ph.D. diss, University of Pennsylvania, Philadelphia, 1969.

Fane, Diana. "The Language of Things: Stewart Culin as Collector." In *Objects of Myth and Memory: American Indian Art at the Brooklyn Museum,* edited by Diana Fane et al., 13–18. New York, 1991.

Hale, Grace Elizabeth. *Making Whiteness. The Culture of Segregation in the*

South, 1890–1940. Ph.D. diss, Rutgers University, New Brunswick, 1995.

Harvey, Byron, III. "The Fred Harvey Collection, 1899–1963." *Plateau* 36 (1963): 33–53.

Higham, John. "The Reorientation of American Culture in the 1890s." In *The Origins of Modern Consciousness,* edited by John Weiss, 25–48. Detroit, 1965.

Hinsley, Curtis M., Jr. "Ethnographic Charisma and Scientific Routine." In *Observers Observed: Essays on Ethnographic Fieldwork,* edited by George W. Stocking, Jr., 53–69. Madison, 1983.

———. "Zunis and Brahmins: Cultural Ambivalence in the Gilded Age." In *Romantic Motives: Essays on Anthropological Sensibility,* edited by George W. Stocking, Jr., 169–207. Madison, 1989.

Holmes, William Henry. "In Memoriam: Matilda Coxe Stevenson." *American Anthropologist,* n.s., 18 (1916): 552–59.

Holmes, William Henry, et al. "In Memoriam: Frank Hamilton Cushing." *American Anthropologist,* n.s., 2 (1900): 354–80.

Jacknis, Ira. "Franz Boas and Exhibits: On the Limitations of the Museum Method of Anthropology." In *Objects and Others: Essays on Museums and Material Culture,* edited by George W. Stocking, Jr., 75–111. Madison, 1985.

———. "Franz Boas and Photography." *Studies in Visual Communication* 10 (1984): 2–60.

———. "The Road to Beauty: Stewart Culin's American Indian Exhibitions at the Brooklyn Museum." In *Objects of Myth and Memory: American Indian Art at the Brooklyn Museum,* edited by Diana Fane et al., 29–44. New York, 1991.

Jefferson, Thomas. *Notes on the State of Virginia,* in *The Portable Thomas Jefferson,* edited by Merrill D. Peterson, 23–29. New York, 1975.

Kirshenblatt-Gimblett, Barbara. "Objects of Ethnography." In *Exhibiting Cultures: The Poetics and Politics of Museum Display,* edited by Ivan Karp and Steven D. Lavine, 386–443. Washington, D.C., 1991.

Lurie, Nancy Oestreich. "Women in Early American Anthropology." In *Pioneers of American Anthropology: The Uses of Biography,* edited by June Helm [McNeish], 31–81. Seattle, 1966.

Mason, Otis T. "Ethnological Exhibit of the Smithsonian Institution at the World's Columbian Exposition." In *Memoirs of the Inter-*

national Congress of Anthropology, edited by C. Staniland Wake, 208–16. Chicago, 1894.

———. "The Occurance of Similar Inventions in Areas Widely Apart." *Science* 9 (1887): 534–35.

Parezo, Nancy J. "Matilda Coxe Evans Stevenson." In *Women Anthropologists: A Biographical Dictionary*, edited by Ute Gacs et al., 337–43. New York, 1988.

Rodgers, Daniel T. "In Search of Progressivism." *Reviews in American History* 10 (1982): 113–32.

Stepan, Nancy Leys. "Race and Gender: The Role of Analogy in Science." *Isis* 77 (1986): 261–76.

Tylor, Edward B. "How the Problems of American Anthropology Present Themselves to the English Mind." *Science* 4 (1884): 545–51.

Weigle, Marta. "From Desert to Disney World." *Journal of Anthropological Research* 45 (Spring 1989): 115–37.

Weinberger, Eliot. "The Camera People." *Transition: An International Review* 55 (1992): 24–55.

Woodward, Arthur. "Frank Cushing—'First War-Chief of Zuni.' " *Masterkey* 13 (1939): 172–79.

INDEX

—〰—